Tent Pegs
and
2nd Lieutenants

Tent Pegs
and
2nd Lieutenants

Memoirs and Stories of the
Korean War

John W. Harper

Illustrations by
Douglas S. Allen

Conversation Press, Inc.
Winnetka, Illinois

As outlined in the Preface, *Tent Pegs and 2nd Lieutenants* is a combination of memoir and fiction. The actions and behavior of people in the stories are purely a product of the author's imagination, and should not be attributed to any real persons, living or dead.

Tent Pegs and 2nd Lieutenants is not an official publication of nor endorsed by the United States Marine Corps.

ISBN 0-9634395-7-X (hardcover)
ISBN 0-9634395-8-8 (paperback)

To Captain Herbert M. Anderson, How Company,
Third Battalion, First Marines and the twenty other
officers and men of the Battalion killed in action
September 1951.

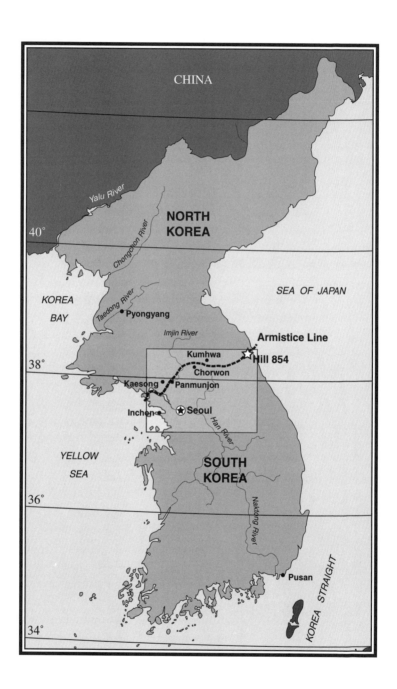

Contents

Illustrations
by Douglas S. Allen

Acknowledgments

My late father, Paul C. Harper, wore sergeant's stripes in the National Guard's First Illinois Cavalry in 1916. Demobilized from the Guard in 1917, he went to France as an Army Field Artillery captain in World War I, and to the West Pacific in World War II as a lieutenant colonel in the Marine Corps Artillery. Having been under shot and shell from an assortment of enemies, he understood whereof I wrote in uncensored letters to him from Korea. He relayed my war letters to *LIFE Magazine* in 1951. *LIFE* published them that year, and later in book form, *Great Reading from LIFE*. Excerpts from the latter are included in a chapter here. This early encouragement started me rewriting my Korean War experiences into memoirs and short stories.

My brother, Paul C. Harper, Jr., Major, USMCR (Ret.), took time from his painting and his own writing to edit and critique the material here. He has published his memoirs of the assaults against Kwajalein, Saipan, Tinian and Iwo Jima in World War II.

An artillery officer, he earned the Bronze Star medal for gallantry during the fight for Saipan.

An ally who aided and abetted in rewriting the memoir chapters is Joseph D. Reed, Major, USMCR (Ret.). He recalled details of the fight for Hill 854, described in the title memoir, some of which I had forgotten. He revealed other details not known to me until we met again forty-five years later. On September 20, 1951, then 2nd Lieutenant Reed led the bayonet charge described in the title chapter.

The ink sketches are by Douglas S. Allen. Douglas took time from a full schedule of painting and showings to create the illustrations. His action scenes included here are based on photographs of the war. His credentials include studies under Oskar Kokoschka in Salzburg and Switzerland. He has shown his paintings and sketches in Paris, Honfleur, Luxembourg, Switzerland, Palm Beach and Chicago. He holds the award, *Chevalier de L'Ordre Francais des Arts et Lettres*.

Instructors from the Northwestern University School of Continuing Studies edited and critiqued the manuscript, and stayed on my case to make sure that I applied their teachings of clarity, style and grammar.

An important source of encouragement came from the organization of the veterans of How Company, Third Battalion, First Marine Regiment. Roughly every three months, it sends newsletters and membership data to its subscribers. The lists include the names and addresses of all responding Marines carried on the How Company rosters between 1950 and 1955. The organization holds annual reunions at various United States locations. The half-century since they fought together hasn't changed their collective will to hang together and hang tough. Given comradeship and mutual support that strong, what chances did the North Korean Peoples Army and the Chinese Communist Forces ever have taking the field to fight them?

Preface

This book is a series of memoirs and short stories based on recollections of actual events and personalities from the Korean War. The memoirs are presented as other participants and I recall them. The short stories reschedule or reposition or aggregate observed incidents and actual personalities. My thought is that the stories have the same feel as my actual experiences or the events I watched taking place. The last piece is included to refresh memories or put back into perspective the history, in broad strokes, of how the Korean War came about and proceeded and ended, though, in fact, it has never ended.

"Up to the Front" is a memoir of my first hours on the front line facing the North Korean Peoples Army.

"Displaced Persons" and "Comfort Woman" are stories based on actual events in which I was involved but which took place in different circumstances or sequences. Readers can assume the third person narrating is 1st Lt. Harper, USMCR, regardless of the name assigned.

" 'But That Was in Another Country: and Besides . . . ' " is also an aggregate of separate events I saw or participated in or heard talked about.

The title piece, "Tent Pegs and 2nd Lieutenants," and "Medical Company" are memoir descriptions of events and my involvement in them. These recollections remain extremely vivid.

"Under Fire" is war reporting. I wrote it at the front a few days after the mayhem or comedy described. It is part of a letter to my father which *LIFE* Magazine printed and *Great Reading from Life* reprinted, without further editing. As I wrote it, I still felt the warrior's reason for being, to engage and destroy the enemy. My excitement while putting pen to paper overpowered hard-won grammar lessons, even literacy. The English grammar teachers and professors who prodded me along to diplomas and who later read the piece, may have developed second, unprintable thoughts for whatever passing grades they had given me.

I wrote the piece from *LIFE* fifty years ago, the year it was published. It is, again, unedited from its original wording. It contains terms and designations not acceptable today. I have not changed them to conform to 21st century sensitivities. It was the lingo of the troops then fighting against the North Korean Peoples Army and the Chinese Communist Forces. It reflects attitudes created by the two major, bloody, Asian wars the U.S. fought in the decade which included the article's writing. The language belongs in reporting those wars because it is part of those wars.

"First to Fight" is a short story driven by the opinion of a "front-liner," which I consider myself to have been, of how regimental staff officers spent their time. It is *not* based on actual events or operations. It describes only how I perceive certain real personalities might have interacted if they had been collected into one command staff and ordered to direct a fight against the North Korean Peoples Army.

The trial of combat, being under fire, can stress anyone trying to describe or convey the experience into a temporary hallucination. The experiences, privation and exertion and fear are unfamiliar and unreal; they are rattling and distorting because of their power and violence and outcome. Living in hostile, unreal, remote circumstances isolates and disconnects.

Descriptions of those experiences, therefore, don't have conventional structure. They don't have organized beginnings, middle parts and endings. They have only middle parts. The author/participant starts his story after the full story has begun, in its middle, when he gets thrown into the fight. He ends his story when someone breaks off the fight, or he gets taken to a field hospital for repairs, or he goes home.

Finally, I generally do not use people's actual names, except in instances where I believe the individuals deserve the recognition. The assigned names are not meant to protect the innocent. None of us qualified as such for long.

The Acknowledgments pages may suggest that my family are Marine Corps janissaries, or tried to be. This is not my intent, and we are not. Genealogical records state that an ancestor took part in amphibious operations 709 years before the Continental Marines opened shop in Tun's Tavern. They indicate that an ancestor sailed with William, The Bastard, of Normandy in his 1066 AD amphibious assault against England. The records also suggest that ancestor to have been a *chevalier*, a medieval "front-liner." Much later, a Harper ancestor fought against the French for George II and George III in the American Colonies. His two sons fought for George Washington against George III. A namesake great grandfather fought for Robert E. Lee. The ancestral warriors may have shown some fickleness or opportunism in their allegiances, but they have almost always thrown in with the winners.

JOHN W. HARPER
2001

1
Introduction

As listed in the chronology at the end of this introduction, the Korean War began on June 25, 1950, when the North Korean Peoples Army invaded South Korea. The most dramatic events all took place within the first year of fighting, leading too many people to believe that there was no real war thereafter. Nothing could be farther from the truth. Thousands on both sides were killed and wounded during the following two-plus years, as real estate changed hands and the armies battled for a position of strength to take to the armistice negotiating tables during the interminable "peace" talks.

These memoirs and stories begin in July 1951, when I joined the First Marine Division in North Korea. During the preceding period of April, May and June, the Division had been in continuous action against the attacking Chinese Communist Forces and the North Korean Peoples Army. The Marine Division was part of the United Nations forces, which had defeated and forced into retreat this third powerful offensive by the Communist armies.

In July, the respective armies had stabilized their front lines while attempting "cease-fire and armistice" talks.

In August, 1951, the negotiations fell apart. The United Nations forces resumed their attacks deeper into North Korea. Within months, the attacks forced the Communist armies to resume negotiations. By late 1951, both armies had assumed static, "stand-off" postures.

Korean War Chronology

June 25, 1950	North Korean Peoples Army invades South Korea.
June 28, 1950	NKPA captures Seoul, capital of South Korea.
August 1, 1950	United Nations forces driven to within miles of Port of Pusan, nearly losing the remaining supply and seaport facility.
September 15-28, 1950	UN forces land at Inchon, near Seoul; recapture Seoul, collapsing North Korean invasion.
September 30, 1950	UN forces begin to drive NKPA to extreme north of North Korea.
October 19, 1950	UN forces capture Pyongyang, capital of North Korea.
October 25-30, 1950	UN forces encounter first Chinese Communist Forces troops, which then drive UN from Yalu River.
December 5, 1950	CCF recaptures Pyongyang.
December 25, 1950	CCF drives UN forces back across the 38th Parallel.
January 4, 1951	UN evacuates Seoul.
February 15, 1951	CCF's drive south stopped.
March 15, 1951	UN retakes Seoul.

Korean War Chronology (continued)

April 3, 1951	UN crosses 38th Parallel moving north.
April 22, 1951	CCF begins spring offensive.
April 24, 1951	UN withdraws from "Iron Triangle" (Pyongyang, Chorwon and Kumwha).
April 29, 1951	CCF attempt to cross Han River repulsed by UN.
May 23, 1951	CCF dig in to build underground defenses along 38th Parallel.
June 12, 1951	UN controls "Iron Triangle" sector.
July 10, 1951	First armistice negotiations begin at Kaesong.
August 23, 1951	Armistice negotiations collapse, fighting resumes, including "Bloody Ridge" and "Heartbreak Ridge."
August 31, 1951	UN forces, including First Marine Division, press attacks into North Korea.
October 15, 1951	"Heartbreak Ridge" captured by UN.
October 25, 1951	Cease-fire talks resume at Panmunjon.
November 17, 1951	38th Parallel agreed upon as line of demarcation.
June 23, 1952	UN bombs Yalu River power plants.

July-August, 1952	Fighting continues. Heavy Marine casualties at Bunker Hill.
August 29, 1952	Intense air raid launched against Pyongyang.
April 26, 1953	Armistice negotiations become serious.
May 28-June 30, 1953	CCF attack U.S. 25th Division, ROK troops near Jumsong and U.S. I Corps.
June 17, 1953	Revised demarcation line agreed to.
July 27, 1953	Armistice signed at Panmunjon. Permanent Peace Treaty never signed.

2

Up to the Front

NORTH KOREA
JULY 1951

I don't recall boarding the cargo plane. I nursed a strep fever virulent enough to earn an offer of a sickbay bed in Pusan, South Korea. An early morning prescribed aureomycin dose left me addled before and during the flight. Navy doctors diagnosed the infection genuine, not malingering, and not due to my own misconduct. But staying behind sick didn't look right, and I had gotten myself onto a flight north with thirty enlisted men. We belonged to a draft of a thousand replacements, all fresh from the U.S., being flown or motored north to the First Marine Division. The Division had been deployed in contact with the North Korean Peoples Army since February.

The flight might have taken an hour. I dozed through it, slumped in a storage cubicle designed for something other than groggy lieutenants. The deferential flight crew offered the privacy since I appeared more boozed and hungover than feverish. They assumed I couldn't face the home stretch into the war unless half drunk.

A crewman shook me back to consciousness with a tactful offer.

"We're coming into K46, Hoengsong, Lieutenant, if you want to watch the landing." A polite hint to "Pull yourself together! You're about to go to war!"

I got myself standing and lurched to the cockpit door. The plane had nosed down and rolled into a steep bank. Looking forward through the windshield, all I could see were pine woods and steep ridges. At the controls, the joking pilot and co-pilot occasionally looked forward at the same. The diving turn and laughing continued as the trees and ridges got closer. Someone had misplaced K46, or the aircrew was playing a convincing trick on the tenderfoot. Altitude dropping, the bank got steeper and the turn harder; but still no airfield. When the treetops reached to where the wing tip had to be, the aircraft snapped to level. The airstrip panned in front of and swept under the windshield. The wheels thumped onto a bumpy, twice fought-over airstrip K46.

The plane bounced to woods at the strip end and spun around facing in the direction it had landed. A crew sergeant slammed open the cargo doors. Someone on the ground threw a wooden ramp up against the jam. "All right! Everybody out! Everybody out! Move out! Out! Out! Move out! Out!" The troops unstrapped themselves and crowded out the door. I grabbed my pack and carbine and stumbled down the ramp after them, getting out of the way of thirty veteran Marines charging into the plane, overjoyed to be on their way back to the U.S. on their own feet, not on stretchers or in plastic bags.

The veterans loaded, the ramp flung aside and the cargo doors slammed shut, the engines revved blowing exhaust and a gravel shower at us. The plane accelerated and lifted away back toward Pusan with its whooping cargo.

A corporal ordered the enlisted passengers onto a truck. A jeep driver welcomed me, and seemed to know where to take me.

"How was the flight, Lieutenant? Anybody shoot at you on the way—I mean guerrillas?"

"I don't think so."

How would I have known? I was goddamn drugged asleep and didn't know or care if guerrillas shot at us; if they had, they missed. The question explained the pilot's hotdog approach onto the airstrip; he would not offer himself to guerrilla antiaircraft fire as a big, slow, low-flying target.

I felt as if I were running on antibodies. If my detachment struck the veteran driver as rank-consciousness or autism, I didn't care about that either; or about the bullet hole through the windshield.

We drove through woods to Regimental and then Battalion Headquarters. A clerk joined me into the Battalion roster; the adjutant assigned me to Rifle Company How, and told me how I would get there.

"How Company is up on the hill. The corporal here will drive you to where the supply trail starts. Private Wilkins will guide you from there, up the hill to How Company."

"Don't go getting lost, Wilkins," the clerk admonished. "Not a chance. Not a chance," Wilkins guaranteed, as if the two were in on something.

They were "in on" the height and pitch of the hill, and the physical condition of replacements from the States. An Eastern Korean hill is a high, narrow mountain ridge, pine covered and steeply sloped, one of which we brushed flying into K46. The front lines extended along the tops of ridges at two to three thousand feet. Replacements climbed the unrelenting gradients to reach the lines. A topographic map, made by the Imperial Japanese army when it occupied Korea , would show the point where the jeep dropped us at 400 meters altitude; How Company and the front were at 700 meters, a climb of about one thousand feet.

I had taken another dose of aureomycin undiluted by the prescribed, but now unavailable, water chasers. Aching, feverish, out of condition and zonked by the drug, I carried a carbine, a pistol, bullets for both, two water canteens, C Rations, a sleeping bag and ground sheet, a shelter-half, a poncho, extra clothing, toilet articles, and two fifths of bourbon. Veterans unofficially urged replacement officers to bring the last items as ex-voto offerings to their new, usually skeptical and always thirsty comrades.

When we reached the base of the ridge, the jeep driver grinned, "Good luck, Lieutenant." I adjusted my pack and carbine and belt as the driver rattled his jeep back toward Regimental comfort.

Our conditioning for the last month had included three weeks sardined in a troop ship, two days and nights of debauchery in Tokyo, four days of leisure in replacement and transient camps. Soft and sick and carrying every front line living necessity, I looked at the one-thousand-foot climb paced by a lean, healthy, unburdened nineteen-year-old. He would have great fun making a commissioned officer miserable, guiding him up the hill until the officer reached the top, or gave up and collapsed, or turned back and deserted.

"Here's the trail, Lieutenant. Ready to move out?" Wilkins asked politely, hoping I would ask for a break to make my peace before he started having fun.

"Let's go."

I had to keep pace with Wilkins. I resolved not to stop for a break unless he stopped. The packed gravel trail offered solid footing. Switchbacks eased the pitch, the trail a zigzag shelf following less unforgiving grades. Fever, antibiotics, non-condition, equipment load, the continuous pitch, the height and the goddamn taunting nimbleness of Private Wilkins all reinforced my resolve. Within yards I began measuring the climb in gasps, not steps. One foot in front of the other, one switchback after another; the ridge seemed without a crest. Wilkins trotted while I plodded. The trail would not relent; it kept on and up, switching left and right, forever. Wilkins bounded ahead mercilessly. I felt that something inside me would snap; all I could do was to gasp and plod until I blacked out and dropped.

I sensed that there was more sky and less ridge side above and ahead; stunted pines and brush hinted we were closing the ridge top. The trail stopped switching, leveling to a berm leading in one direction. Brush and undergrowth gave way to piles of freshly dug earth and footpaths.

A bearded, scowling figure in dungarees coated by red earth stood up out of nowhere.

"Wilkins, what you got there?"

"The new lieutenant."

"How does he look?"

"Pretty tender."

The figure dropped out of sight. I took the barb and continued one foot in front of the other. Wilkins strode ahead.

The berm stayed level along the side of the ridge. I caught my breath and took in more of where I was. If this was the goddamn front line, where were its goddamn defenders?

"Here's the Company CP, Lieutenant. Captain Henderson's bunker is the one with the skull stuck up on the post. Enjoyed the climb." Wilkins took his parting shot and dropped out of sight into another bunker.

I approached Captain Henderson's ossuary under its grinning totem. The skull wore a North Korean Army field cap and a natty blue bandana tied to a stick where its vertebrae had been. I spoke Henderson's name into the mouth of his bunker. He crawled out smiling, shaven, clean, and introduced himself.

"Harper! John? Welcome to the war! We've been waiting for you! Wilkins didn't give you the scenic route, did he? Or did he? ExO, meet John Harper, our replacement for Tom Watts. John, this is Jim Carr, our Executive Officer. That's First Sergeant Smith over there behind the big beard, the Old Man of the Mountain. Corporal Ames, take Lieutenant Harper over to Lieutenant Watts' area. John, you'll be taking over Watts' Platoon. Tom will get you settled somewhere and orient you. You and Tom come back at chow time. We're having a birthday party for Lieutenant Robbins. He's just turned twenty three. The birthday boy is all grown up now. He says he might up and join the United States Marines one of these days. See you around 1600. You can meet the other officers then. Glad to have you aboard!"

Other heads poked up from bunkers like wolves from dens sizing up fresh meat. So far nothing made sense. Wilkins had tried to run me into the ground. Henderson acted as if I were joining a fraternity. The bug-eyed First Sergeant had a gray beard so full it belonged in a theatrical supply store. The ExO smiled too much. Now, they're throwing a birthday party! Where was the goddamn war with its shot and shell and bloodletting and heroics?

Ames led me along the wooded ridge top toward Watts' Platoon area. The path followed the front line, which showed no signs of enemy malice; no shell craters or shattered trees or smashed defense works, no stench of uninterred flesh; only scattered trenches and foxholes in pine woodland.

We found Watts digging another hole. He spoke in a back country whine, his head jerked in a tick. I disliked him on sight. I told myself I would get over it; I never did. He pointed to the reverse slope where he said I would find an unused foxhole, promised an orientation later, then went back to his digging. Ames left for the Command Post. I made my way down the slope to find the promised foxhole and set up housekeeping.

I began feeling less sick and wobbly. The excitement of being "in the front lines" overrode the washed out sensation. The guest foxhole, dug into the south slope of the ridge, faced away from the North Korean Army lines two thousand yards north. In defilade behind the front line ridge top, the opposition couldn't see me or fire directly at me. I would be able to join the hostilities gradually. The foxhole had been dug horizontally, long enough to stretch out in and deep enough to shield against ground explosions and splinters. A tented poncho over it protected the resident from rain; luck had to take over if air or tree bursts of enemy shell fire struck too close. An earlier occupant had left three hand grenades and a full carbine magazine, settling and unsettling for a tenderfoot. They could be a sort of room service, or preparations for a last stand.

Watts arrived to see that I had found my assigned quarters and to size me up. He sat himself on the edge of the foxhole, hanging booted feet into what I already considered my bed. He wore his first lieutenant's bars on his collar, carried a .45 on his hip, a studied "front-liner" except for his camouflaged helmet which didn't seem to fit.

"This foxhole doesn't have overhead cover, just the poncho, but there hasn't been too much 'incoming' for the last two weeks. We've beaten up the North Koreans pretty good. You'll be okay, safe enough here. We shouldn't be here too long, anyway. We should be rotated to the rear soon. We're overdue to be rotated to reserve Battalion."

Watts' head kept twitching, and he worried at a mole or wart on the side of his neck. A black mustache curled over the corners of his mouth giving him a disapproving, menacing look. He scratched his head as if taxed or inconvenienced. He seemed to measure my apparent competence and the state of my nerves, the second suggesting he thought I might panic and bolt off to the rear, marooning him to wait for another relief. The staring, front-line eyes, the mole pinching, the head twitch, the mustache preening, the perched helmet that sat too high and wobbled as he talked and twitched; small wonder that I, or someone, had been sent to relieve him.

He didn't drawl; he mouthed his words. His verbal tactics included stammering or repetition to control the conversation when he ran out of words. Taking me in his sights as a conversational prisoner of war, he started self-promoting and politicking.

"We've got a fairly good team here in my Platoon. I've selected and trained all my non-coms, and I have brought them all to a high state of, well, I'll say steadiness as well as competence. When you take over I think you'll find they're as good, or better, than you'll find anywhere in the Battalion." He detailed the personality and professional traits of each subordinate until I lost track of whom he was evaluating.

Then he addressed the other officers' qualifications and fitness; the Company Commander and the Executive Officer, the machine gun and mortar officers, the two other rifle Platoon officers. He gave them all grades of average or below. One of the rifle Platoon leaders had been highly decorated, a detail omitted from his appreciation. A gabby, transparent manipulator, Watts lived in the first person singular.

He noticed a non-regulation bulge in my knapsack and guessed I had brought euphoriants.

"You didn't happen to bring some bourbon up with you, by any chance, did you?"

He had me, goddamn him! "Sure. Get yourself a cup."
"I'll do that. You got some water left to cut it with, I
expect?"
"Yes. Give me a few more minutes here to get organized."
Watts hustled away while I dug one fifth out of my knapsack and buried the second deeper. I had doubts about mix-
ing Seagrams and aureomycin with a fever on an empty
stomach, but the option had been taken away. Watts
returned in minutes with his canteen cup and his thirst,
smiling at the thought of tossing off low-end 80-proof cut
with warm, heavily chlorinated water.

"The First Battalion seems to be the regimental palace
guard. They've been in reserve for the last month. We've
been up here while they relax back there. I can't figure out
who's so friendly with whom, they get to stay in the rear so
long."

I wanted to know about the opposition training their
guns on us from a few thousand yards north, when and
where How Company's last fire fight had taken place. Had
How Company taken this ridge? Watts was fixated on getting himself to the rear, away from the front. I wondered
what he thought he had hired out to do when he joined the
Marines.

"Well, let's have one for the road, and we'll go see what
kind of birthday celebration they've got cooked up for young
Lieutenant Robbins."

What had been cooked up had actually been mailed to
Lieutenant Robbins and had arrived unplundered: a small
birthday cake decorated with its caring message and the
number 23 in icing. Using his bayonet, Robbins cut it carefully into seven pieces and served the treats on pieces of letter paper. The cake tasted sweet if not bakery-fresh. The
thoughtful, homey celebration seemed something of a taunt
this close to a desperate enemy. Only treetops masked us
from his line of sight and fire.

A North Korean artilleryman had spotted something else
that irked him. The muzzle blast of his ranging shot made

an authoritative "pop" from the distance, followed by the signature whistle of its 76-millimeter shell. He intended the fire to break up a laundry party in a stream below us and a half-mile to our right. We didn't spot his chosen target until we heard the round land, and we had picked ourselves up from the dirt. The birthday party had been a good idea, anyway. The artillery fire ended it, and we all went back to ground—Watts and me to my warm Seagrams and chlorine.

Darkness stopped the digging and bantering and drinking; the whole front went quiet. Watches took their posts. Searchlights miles to our rear trained beams forward and upward, the light reflecting downward off cloud cover; "artificial moonlight" illumination to reveal sneak attacks. Within minutes of full darkness, 81-millimeter and 4.2 inch mortars behind us began intermittent salvos of "harassing and interdictory" fire onto favored approaches to our lines. The 81s' muzzle blasts made clunks, and their shells hissed as they passed overhead; the 4.2s' firing made louder barks, and their shells whistled. Reassured by the alert, belligerent defenses, exhausted and feverish, Seagrams and aureomycin sedated, I took to my sleeping bag. The war in good hands, I didn't wake up until full daylight.

Watts sent a runner to invite me to his bunker for breakfast coffee, and to determine if I had stayed on board and in place over night, or had lost my nerve and sneaked away to the rear and safety.

3
Displaced Persons

NORTH KOREA

JULY 1951

Lieutenant Howard saw them as so many beauties. Dusty, smoking, jolting General Motors six-by-six trucks would rumble out of the woods to take him and the whole Battalion away from front-line discomfort, alarms, and danger. He watched the column of Detroit's fairest turn slowly into the Battalion staging park, circle and stop bumper to bumper. Sergeants yelled out vehicle assignments; then the whole Battalion scrambled aboard, thirty-plus whooping and bantering troops squeezing into each truck.

All loaded, the convoy commander signaled the drivers to pull away. Engines revving, gears crunching, the column recircled the staging park, turned out onto the main supply route and headed south toward safety and the comfort of tents overhead, cots for sleeping and three cooked meals every day.

Lieutenant Howard boarded the lead truck of the two carrying his Platoon. His rank commanded him the passenger seat next to the driver.

Howard greeted the driver, Private First Class Andrews, settled himself and looked ahead through a bullet hole in the windshield. North Korean and Chinese snipers fired exclusively at passengers through vehicles' windshield glass, their points of aim and marksmanship curiously uniform, always leaving the bullet holes and spider-web fractures in passengers' faces. They never shot into the glass on the driver's side or its edge or frame. Above the punctured windshield, Pfc. Andrews flaunted the best in combat blazonry; a human skull stuck on a mop handle. The skull's absent jawbone and missing teeth gaps implied its decapitation in a desperate *mano a mano* somewhere. Whether the skull had belonged to an allied or enemy soldier, or male or female bystander, Andrews' *fasces* announced him as a rampaging warrior. The death's-head threat: "Look what happened to the last guy who messed with me!"

Entertained by Andrews' battlefield theater, Howard asked, "Were you here last winter?"

"Andrews meant to horrify anyone."

"Yes, Sir. That I was."

"Up north with Colonel Puller?"

"Yes, Sir. He got us out, somehow. Had a close call, though. A mine blew the front wheels off my truck. Lifted me right out of it, too. I was carrying a load of dead guys; frozen stiff. They got dumped all over the road. Colonel Puller ordered every one of them brought out with us. So we did, most of them."

A bullet hole at his face, someone's skull flaunted overhead, tales of mine blasts and flying wreckage and a truckload of frozen cadavers tumbling onto a road, Andrews meant to horrify Howard or anyone else who didn't know better. Howard kept a straight face.

"Did it get you a Purple Heart?"

"No, Sir. Just bandages and another six-by-six—this one here."

Howard thought for a few seconds, then with manufactured unease, "We'll drive carefully today, anyway, won't we?"

Andrews laughed. "Yes, Sir!"

The convoy had the supply route to itself; no other traffic, no civilians. The trucks turned left around a hill, then took a gradual right curve showing Howard the full truck column and gravel road for hundreds of yards ahead. He saw a Korean woman sitting on the road shoulder, bending forward holding her head in her hands as if weeping. A cloth sling bag hung from a shoulder. A small child stood beside her, watching the stream of trucks rumbling within feet, drafting dust and spraying gravel. Howard heard the troops calling out, "Hey, Mama-san, pogey bait! Boy-san! Candy, boy-san!" as they pelted the two with candy bars. The exhausted, wrung-out woman and her child didn't move or react to the roaring convoy or to the feast of calories tossed around them.

Howard had never paid attention to the officialese, "collateral casualties." The woman had been chased out of a

wrecked home and overrun village. She had carried her
child and a few necessities away from the fighting into alien
geography until she collapsed. She had nowhere and no one
to go to, easy pickings for bandits and rogue soldiery.

Howard reconsidered the skull fixed to the mop handle
top, wondering what particular violence had been done to
the woman's parents, husband, siblings, other children.
How much strength and will did she have left?

4

"But That Was in Another Country: and Besides..."

SOUTH KOREA

JULY 1951

The truck convoy had brought us south from the front to our rest camp. The farmer who had worked our Company area had planted it in corn, by hand, hill by hill, in time to be expropriated. The supply people had dumped our tents next to the corn patch turned camp area. They had also dropped off poles to raise the tents. They did not inventory the support posts and bars needed to stretch the tents into shelters. These would be our problem. We had neither saws nor axes to chop the pine trees above our corn patch. We attacked the stunted trees with entrenching tools and returned to set up the needed supports before nightfall.

Fortunate timing; the last of the monsoon cloudbursts broke that night. We spent the next morning gouging drainage gutters around the tents, all of which had been flooded muddy by the rains.

The Battalion mess kitchen had been set up and was running. Personal hygiene seemed a logical next step. Some of the troops hadn't had a bath of any description for weeks, except while marching or standing watch under the monsoons.

A channeled tributary of a river flowed three hundred yards north of the camp. The Battalion had been allocated late afternoon hours to wash itself off in the channel. Some nine hundred of us marched to it, strung ourselves out along the muddy bank, tossed our dungarees and skivvies in dirty piles and waded naked into the soupy, knee-deep water.

Upstream, the channel had been sluiced to irrigate a chain of rice paddies. The flowage spread over the terraced paddies, warmed, aerated and partly sanitized by ultraviolet rays before draining back into the river. The thrifty farmers working the paddy chain spiked the flowage with barnyard droppings and household night soil. The additives overtasked the ultraviolet rays and aeration. The leisurely current through the rice stalks proved too gentle to break up lumps of ordure. I knew I had returned to the Asian countryside when I felt an excreta lump drift against my leg. The soaping and splashing went on, with appropriate care where we splashed, passing succeeding lumps down the current to the next bathers.

The bathing channel measured twenty or thirty yards wide; a gravel road ran close to its opposite bank. The road joined the main supply route which carried supplies and personnel to and from the front and rear area camps and headquarters.

All nine hundred of us looked up at a jeep bouncing down the road toward us. Nothing unusual about a jeep. This one attracted our attention. It had its canvas roof in place, and it had metal side shields mounted to protect the driver and passenger from splashing and drafts.

When it closed on us bathers, we saw that the jeep carried three Red Cross ladies on their way to discharge their duties, errands of morale-building or beguilement. The time of day being the civilized cocktail hour, someone of rank and station had requested their company. The politesse of a written "Requests the Pleasure of your Company" had probably been streamlined to a telephoned, "Send 'em over."

However delivered, the invitation had put the ladies on the road just in time to see our ablutions. How else to get themselves to their party? The only route took them past a bathing party of nine hundred nude Marines. Without towels or clothing or places to hide, standing in water not deep or sanitary enough to flop into, modesty was out of our reach. What could we do but smile and wave and send kisses? What could they do but laugh and wave back to us as they trooped the naked Battalion line, right flank to left, and continue on to their party?

They were the last Occidental women I would see for the next six months.

The incident entertained most of us. One Lieutenant Thompson, however, had been in the boondocks longer than he thought he deserved. The occurrence stirred him more than it should have.

"I'm a passionate man, I tell you, John! I'm a passionate man!"

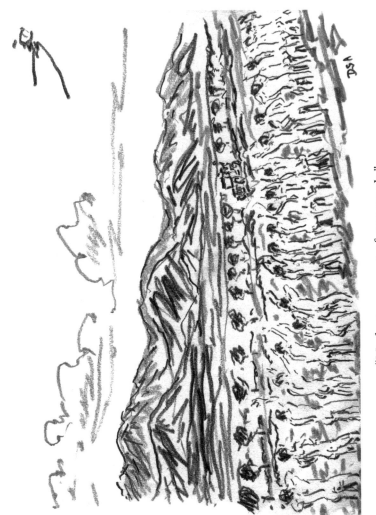

"Modesty was out of our reach."

"I don't have any suggestions for you, Thom. I think we're all stuck here. There aren't enough ladies to go around."

"I'm a passionate man, John! I . . . am . . . a . . . *passionate* . . . man!"

Looking to the future, Thompson saw a bleak social season ahead; a season that needed fixing.

"I think I'll get out my last khaki shirt and get that washee-washee kid that came around the Company, get him to wash it fresh. Then I'll go up the stream to that farm, the one we saw from the trucks coming down, and see if I can't find me a little old 'farmer's daughter.' "

Thompson found the washee-washee kid and gave him the shirt and a used bar of soap, the latter's remnant to be the *quid pro quo* for his laundry service. The washee-washee showed up the next day with Thompson's laundered and neatly folded shirt, leaving it with a sergeant on duty. Thompson reappeared while washee-washee made the rounds of the Company drumming up more laundry business.

"Lieutenant Thompson, the washee-washee kid left your shirt here. It's on the gun box over there."

The closer Thompson got himself to his hymeneal shirt, the worse his distress.

"What . . . how could . . . where did . . . ?" Thompson wailed, "Washee-washee! You get over here! Why didn't you use soap, all that soap I gave you? What did you wash this in? You must have washed it in cow shit! It smells like cow shit!"

Washee-washee saw his laundry client ready to boot him out of the camp, canceling more laundry clients and other lucrative services. He stood his professional ground. "Use tocsan soap! Tocsan soap!" (Much soap.)

"Wash it again in soap, Goddamn it! Soap! Much soap! Tocsan soap!" Thompson made scrubbing motions across the shirt.

"Okay! Okay! Washee ichi-bon! Ichi-bon! (carefully) Okay!"

Washee-washee retreated out of sight to find a better laundry facility, a puddle removed from a cow yard.

"Goddamn! I got to get that shirt back before yesterday's bath wears off me. Timing's everything in these things! Damn! Will he ever get that shirt clean again?"

I tried to comfort and encourage Thompson. "Well, droppings of any kind are always water-soluble. If the water he chooses has less in it than the shirt has—that's a big *if*—it should clean up okay."

A deeply troubled Lt. Thompson walked away repeating, "I'm a passionate man . . . a passionate man . . . cow shit in my only dress-up shirt!"

The duty sergeant, resigned to field sanitation difficulties in the Third World, had gotten a whiff of the problem shirt and predicted, "Whoever she is won't care. She'll smell the same as the shirt."

Washee-washee reappeared the next afternoon with his best effort neatly folded, showing his best sales presence, obeisant but confident. Thompson sniffed his haberdashery and approved, and came up with another used soap bar as a tip to show no hard feelings for yesterday's enormity.

"Why didn't he get it right the first time? Yesterday, I thought I'd have to burn the goddamn shirt!"

After supper, Thompson presented himself at Company Headquarters tent, in moderately clean dungaree pants, cap at a cavalier angle, shaved, khaki shirt almost odorless.

"Now, Thompson, you get yourself back here by sundown, you hear? Or I'll give you such a licking you'll never forget," said his Company Commander playing protective surrogate Mama.

"Captain, I hear you loud and clear, and I assure you I shall obey both the spirit and the letter of your order. 'I shall return!' "

Assuming the moral high ground, I suggested a protocol item. "You better take some money, too, so the family doesn't get the wrong idea; you know, that your intentions aren't honorable."

"Good thinking, John, and I thank you for your concern. I am well financed."

Moving to lower ground, I suggested, "Thompson, have you brought along your . . . 'special equipment?' It's best to protect oneself in these adventures, these 'affairs of the heart,' in far off, exotic lands such as these."

"Lieutenant Thompson is always prepared for the ladies! I have to be! I just never know when my attentions will be needed—demanded! Now, I am off and away!"

Thompson disappeared in the direction of the river. There, he would turn right and walk the mile up his muddy "street of dreams" to his tryst with his *demoiselle particuliere*. That she could not speak in an alluring French accent was a given. That she had not reached the age of consent and would not for another half dozen years was a second given.

The duty sergeant remarked, "The lieutenant should think twice about going up there. I heard some of the guys from George Company went up there right after we got here. It used to be that officers were ordered not to go to the same cribs as enlisted. If the officers got caught, they got a general court-martial."

I added a medical note. "One of the Navy MDs told me that the "ladies of the evening" out here have diseases that have diseases. Penicillin doesn't work on what they pass around."

"Maybe the doctor just tried to scare you."

"He got it done."

Thompson showed up two hours later.

"How did it go?"

"Yeah! Yeah! Come on! Tell us about her."

Thompson looked grim instead of satisfied. Something on his street of dreams excursion had misfired and badly.

"Come on! Don't keep us waiting! Out with it!"

Thompson spoke slowly. "I'm maybe a hundred yards or so from the house. I stop so I can see what's going on. I make a visual reconnaissance. Mama-san is there at the front door, all stooped over and old looking, really old."

"The hell with Mama-san!"

"What about Cho-Cho San . . . girl-san . . . the broad?"

"Well, Mama-san—her mother, I guess—is at the doorway collecting the money from the guys. They pay her and go inside, and in a few minutes if they aren't back out the door she stamps in and raises hell to make them hurry up! It was a goddamn mass production business—a factory!"

Thompson, the romantic, had been given a lesson in how things were, and were not, in the mysterious Far East.

"So, you gave up on the deal?"

"That isn't all. A young Korean guy shows up and starts shouting at Mama-san, and she's shouting and jabbering back at him. He must have been her son, or the broad's boyfriend, or something. They get louder and louder 'til he throws her down on the deck and goes in the house. There's a big scream and a couple of the guys come running out yelling at everyone to take off—which they do, big time. Now Mama-san is screaming her head off. The young guy must have flipped his switch. He was carrying one of those short hoes they chop those corn patches with. I didn't think about it when he first showed up. I thought he just brought it home from work. He comes back out the door all bloody— the broad's blood, I guess. I didn't ask questions. I did the fastest 'To the rear, march' you ever saw."

"Mother Fletcher!"

"Did anyone see you?" I asked.

"I don't think so."

"Did you recognize any of our guys?"

"No."

"The locals will try to pin this on one of us to squeeze money out of us and spare their own kind, if they can."

"I didn't see any of our guys. If they went there, they may have had their fun, whatever, and got away by the time I got there."

"Let's wait for Battalion or Regiment or the MPs to make the first move on this. If they don't, we won't."

"Mama-San is at the doorway, collecting money
from the guys."

I found myself looking carefully at Thompson's hands and pristine shirt.

"All that trouble getting me a clean shirt, and the broad gets goddamn whacked before I get me a bounce!"

"Waiting for that clean shirt may have saved your ass from Portsmouth Naval brig, or worse, a Korean dungeon. You're home free on this one—not even a dose."

Not consoled, Thompson slouched away to his tent. "I'm a passionate man, a passionate man."

5

Comfort Woman

NORTH KOREA

AUGUST 1951

The Platoon marches in two files down a gravel road. The soldiers carry slung rifles and other weapons, cartridge belts and magazines full; grenades hang from belts or slings and bulge pockets. They all carry knapsacks showing bayonets. The soldiers are dusty and perspiring, but their weapons gleam with lubricants. Their dungarees and helmets are worn as if the march had begun at a parade formation. The back-to-chest interval between each stays uniform. Their discipline makes clear this is one of many such marches in their recent experience. Their rate of march speaks urgency; they have a time rendezvous ahead, a violent one, which will be kept. A lieutenant and a sergeant each lead a file.

"Can we take a break, Lieutenant? It's been almost three hours."

"When the Platoon ahead does. Keep it moving and closed up with them."

"Yes, Sir."

Minutes later, "You said the magic word, Sergeant. The second Platoon is holding up. Signal to stop. Do not fall out!"

Unexpected talking and banter and calls of amusement come from the Platoon ahead.

"Look who's here!"

"Mama-san and junior-san!"

"Let 'em through!"

A Korean woman and her child move cautiously past, between the files. She is short, slight, stooped, worn out. She carries a bag of belongings slung over one shoulder and leads her small child with her free hand, walking steadily, eyes on the road ahead in an attitude of nervousness and submission. Her clothing is complete but loose and revealing. Her life, especially her recent life, has used her up. All her possessions are in her bag and walking at her side.

"Candy, boy-san?"

"Candy, hell! Let's you and me have a little rally, Mama-san! Come on, baby!"

One of the soldiers grabs the woman by the arm to drag her off into the underbrush bordering the road. The lieutenant orders, "Leave her alone, Williams!"

"Come on, bitch! Just time for a quick one!"

"Williams, get back in ranks!"

The woman is squealing and the child wailing, the lieutenant shouting again. Williams doesn't or won't hear.

"Williams! Let her go and get back in ranks!" Williams still won't hear the lieutenant and continues dragging the woman as she squeals and jabbers louder and the child screams.

Sliding his carbine off his shoulder and leveling it from his hip, the lieutenant advances toward Williams. "Back in ranks, Williams! Back in ranks, GODDAMN IT!"

Williams releases the woman, who grasps her child, picks up her bag and walks away quickly, collected, down the files pulling the screaming child. The lieutenant stares Williams down, slowly raising his carbine to vertical, then turns and walks forward to the column head, still tense and angry. He glares back at Williams, then turns to the sergeant who offers the emollient, "The second Platoon's moving out, Lieutenant."

"Move 'em out, Sergeant."

"Some break. Wonder if mama-san makes it through Able Company?"

6

Tent Pegs and
2nd Lieutenants

NORTH KOREA

JULY 1951

The First Marines Regimental Commander himself briefed us when we joined the Marine Division as replacement officers. He presented himself bareheaded, outfitted in a jacket whose sleeves were six inches too short, the trouser legs eight inches too short, scuffed dress shoes in place of field boots, no socks. The Commander, Colonel Wilburt "Big Foot" Brown, a Corps legend and veteran of its fights since Belleau Wood in 1918, projected immense pride in his regiment, the hardened warrior's confidence and professionalism, in spite of his get-up.

"This regiment attacked and overran all the real estate you can see from here. North Koreans, the NKPA, occupied all those ridges until six weeks ago. Now the ridges belong to us, and we can take any other ridges the Division tells us to take.

"Weapons and terrain will always dictate tactics. We're in the Taebaek Mountains here in Eastern Korea. They're steep and rugged; you won't climb a ridge here that's less than one thousand feet higher than your start line. The razorback ridge systems here dictate the tactics, ours and the NKPA's, and the Chinese'.

"You can't use extended formations and flanking movements on these ridges; if you do, you'll send your flank troops and yourselves sliding down the ridge sides into the ravines. Attacks have to be channeled up the approach ridges. The approach tops are narrow and sharply crowned; more edged than rounded, you might say. But their pitch tends to ease up at the critical main ridge tops; that's the high ground, which *you must*, I repeat, *you must take*, and once you take it *you must hold it*!

"When the NKPAs attack you, they'll come up the approach ridges in solid columns, their 'human sea' formation, to try to run over you at night with sheer numbers. When they do, you'll have your own Regimental and Battalion weapons plus the Division artillery to help you hold them off.

"But when you go after them, we'll soften them up first with artillery and air strikes. When you make your assaults, you can expect to engage only your lead squads and platoons at any one time. There won't be room on the ridge top for any unit larger. The lead squads and Platoons are the Tip of the Lance. Since you'll be leading them, you'll be the tip of the Tip of the Lance. Glad to have you aboard. Good luck to you all."

*   *   *   *   *   *

NORTH KOREA

SEPTEMBER 20–21 1951

We had trained all summer until September 6, when the Marine Division had deployed to join the renewed UN attacks into North Korea. Our Battalion had been held in reserve or in support of other attack Battalions the previous fourteen days. The NKPAs still showed fight after weeks of UN and Marine Division attacks. On September 20, our Battalion had been ordered to assault a ridge, officially Hill 854, designated by its height in meters. Our Company would climb it, attack and drive the NKPAs off its top or kill or capture them all, and hold the ridge.

I had command of a rifle Platoon. The coming assault would be my first, if the NKPA rear guard stood its ground. More than a numbered topographic feature, Hill 854 dominated a chain of ridges which formed a natural line of defense in North Korea; a "frontier of state" for whoever held it.

The day of our attack the Company stepped off at a gentlemanly 0800 hours. The gravel road and bright Indian summer day made for good marching. The weather would allow close air support. I hadn't thought about that advantage, but someone else had. The seven- or eight-mile march

"We passed a truck smashed by a land mine."

to the objective would take most of the day, the pace more waiting than marching.

We shuffled through a valley whose people had been herded away into internment camps. Derelict rice terraces lay drained and unrepaired; clusters of mud and thatch houses stood empty and looted and wrecked. Ridge sides walled and narrowed the valley, the landscape pastoral and scenic until midmorning, when we passed a truck smashed by a land mine. The wreckage still smelled of TNT. The blast had blown the front wheels and driver's side door away and splattered the seat with the driver's blood.

Beginning the march, the troops had bantered and joked and complained. The humorists' and dissidents' material soon ran out, the troops turning silent, thinking about something they didn't want to think about. I didn't want to think about it, either. This would be the first time I had to face direct enemy fire.

My thoughts turned inward, then to the route and threats of ambush from the surrounding terraces and woods and ridges, to where the out-of-sight Company Commander and the head of the column had gone, then inward again.

The time of day and the slow approach aggravated misgivings about our future; halts and starts in the march imply leaders' indecision. Late afternoon is not—*is not*—a commander's or his troops' first choice for mounting an assault.

By early afternoon, we began hearing rifle and machine gun fire. A band of shot-up survivors from an ROK (South Korean Army) unit appeared in front of us, straggling toward the rear. Walking wounded grimaced and staggered. Exhausted bearers stumbled and lurched, wrestling with litters fashioned out of tree branches and bloodied ponchos. Telephone wire trussed the litters, securing corpses or groaning wounded. The ROKs had a painful trek ahead; retracing our approach route would bring them neither medical facilities nor the transport to take them there.

Through mid-afternoon we passed under the full three-mile length and menace of our objective, the massif of Hill

854, south end to north end. Shell and bomb fire and napalm had blasted and burned away the pine woods on the ridge top, exposing NKPA bunker mounds and firing ports. The veterans among the troopers remarked on the number and size of the bunkers, which appeared unoccupied. We had been promised that the ROKs held the north end of the ridge top. We were to relieve them and chase the NKPAs off the south end.

We closed a meadow at the north base of the ridge; the lead Platoons and sections crossed it and started climbing the grade without a halt. Time and daylight had become critical. The Battalion medical team had begun setting up shop in the meadow. Its presence demonstrated someone's planning; it also implied something much less settling. I received an order to detach a squad to protect the medical team and its helicopter pad. After earlier casualties, the order reduced my Platoon to under half strength before joining the fight.

Loaded with eighty pounds of food, water, bullets, grenades, weapons, shelter and clothing, we joined the 1,500-foot climb up to the fight. The approach path forced the Company into a single file; the column of 200-plus Marines stretched to over 1,000 yards, under minimal control, vulnerable, slow to assemble, unhandy to maneuver when the fight started. My Platoon brought up the rear of the column. I had been out of contact with the head, the Command, of the column all day. The Company CO would reach the ROKs on the ridge top half an hour before I could.

Gunfire from above escalated. An NKPA Maxim machine gun thumped and a "burp gun" ripped at someone; rifle fire increased. Rifle fire is the telltale of an infantry fight. Its disorder means rival troops are firing at will directly into each other; that the rival commanders are not in charge of the fight; the fight itself has taken charge of the fight.

The path up the ridge side faded to a scrape through brush and boulders and trees, a suspected minefield on the left and a cliff edge on the right. The pitch sometimes forced

"The column stretched to over one thousand yards."

us onto all fours. The unreal exertion and urgency of the crashing fight on the ridge above wiped out feelings and senses. Thoughts shrank to climbing up the next six feet.

The squad leader behind me panted, "Lieutenant, the machine gunners and automatic riflemen can't hardly stay on the trail. Can we hold up?"

"No! I'm damn near out of contact with the Platoon ahead! Close up and keep moving!" I did not want to get separated from the rest of the Company and lost or into a minefield or ambushed. We plodded and clawed and gasped up the trail until we arrived near the top.

Bombardments had blasted a tree line several hundred yards below its top, leaving a scarp of churned gravel above it, trees and brush below. As we cleared the tree line, ROK soldiers whom we had been ordered to relieve began streaming down off the ridge, beaten and running. The ROKs' disintegration invited or could easily produce an unsalvageable disaster; it left the critical ridge top without a defense in place. With the Company still strung out from climbing, not assembled for its assault nor organized for its own defense, a prepared enemy could drive a counterattack into the disarray and retake the whole ridge top.

When I closed the Company with my Platoon, the Company Commander and his Executive Officer had made their plan of attack and issued orders which shuffled the order of battle I expected. With the mortar section set into battery, the machine gunners ready to take firing positions, the two lead platoons had been assembled and given the new orders. The Executive Officer ran down from the crest shouting for my Platoon to drop packs and assemble. Instead of holding my Platoon in support, he ordered me to move it forward immediately to follow the lead Platoon in the throw against the NKPAs on the far side, the west side, of the ridge.

My troops laid out their packs in two rows; the rectangular shapes stenciled with names and serial numbers made me think of headstone rows in a cemetery. I ordered the squads toward the ridge top behind the lead Platoon. I had not been briefed on the lie of the ridge, the enemy strength or defenses, the direction of the assault or the location and breach through a minefield.

The din of firing became deafening. An air strike of Marine fighter-bombers attacked the NKPA strongpoint with machine guns, rockets and napalm. In minutes, before I could close behind them, the lead Platoon Leader, Lieutenant Reed, shouted for his Marines to charge; with a yell they rushed over the crest out of sight.

I shouted for the squads to follow me over the ridge and into the attack, and ran over the ridge top down toward the already blazing fight. The assault route followed a descending ridge, its left a tilted open slope swept by automatic weapons fire, its right a hard slope dropping into a canyon. I led my Platoon down the ridge along its right face. We had no room to maneuver and no natural cover—and no other choice.

The line of attack, the line of the ridge, pointed directly into the eye of the setting sun. Blinded by its glare, I could see only bursts of fire from rifles and machine guns, figures darting and crouching, grenades flashing, clouds of dust and smoke.

My vision bleached black and white, and my range perception went two-dimensional. The fight in front looked like a stage backdrop, all of it in my face and crashing with fire.

An NKPA machine gunner fired a burst at me, the bullets cracking and kicking dirt spouts close beside me. I thought I had hidden myself behind a tree stump, but the gunner was onto me and of a mind to saw me in half. I ran further down the slope closing with the lead Platoon survivors.

"Jesus Christ!" A Marine yelled, pointing ahead down into the valley.

A Marine Corsair climbing upward from the valley over the NKPAs, drove his attack run directly at us, his napalm bomb ready to drop, the radial engine and propeller hub pointing into our faces. Our own air support was taking aim

"The Platoon Leader shouted for his Marines to charge."

to roast us alive with napalm! The Corsair banked left selecting his target in the canyon below us, roared past dropping his napalm and climbing up out of the canyon and over the ridge. Napalm flared and drafted up the canyon in a huge flame curtain.

On the ridge top to the west, the NKPAs wrestled a 76-millimeter cannon out of hiding and into battery; the gunners could see us all and fire directly into their victims of choice. They selected our support and headquarters people above and behind us, opening fire at the ridge top, sending shell after shell screaming overhead, crashing into them. A shell blew off someone's helmet, sending it bounding down the ridge side. I had to wonder if the helmet was empty or contained its late owner's head. The 76 barrage and machine gun and rifle fire crashed and cracked. Within minutes, NKPA rifle fire killed our Company Commander.

*　　*　　*　　*　　*　　*

Minutes before he was to attack, the lead Platoon Commander, Lieutenant Reed, had learned of a minefield in his assault path. The about-to-be-relieved ROK commander, who knew the location of the minefield and the breach through it, was far more interested in living out the day than discussing land mines with his relief. Not getting the information he meant to have, Reed unsheathed his bayonet and made it clear that the ROK Commander would go to the rear in slices if he didn't spell out where the mines were and were not. The ROK officer jabbered and pointed and twitched symbols and markings on a sheet of paper, then bolted away down the ridge.

Reed assembled his troops and led them in a dash over the ridge and down the west slope. Early in the charge he fired an automatic burst from his carbine; the punishing full automatic fire shook his carbine apart into pieces. Armed with a Luger taken in an earlier war, he moved his Platoon 200 yards down the ridge spine.

The NKPAs waited, protected behind a hook in the ridge, armed with a Maxim machine gun, a Degtyarev automatic rifle, grenades and rifles. When the Marines closed, the NKPAs fired into them with weapons enough to kill the whole assault Platoon. Poor sighting of the Maxim and Degtyarev sent their fire high and through gaps in the attack formation. The Platoon charged through the fire to the base of the hook, firing and grenading. NKPA fire killed a senior squad leader. Another sergeant lost a hand throwing back a fused NKPA grenade. Forced back by automatic fire and the grenade barrage, they retrieved their casualties and took what cover they could. Half of the Platoon fell in front of the hook in a few swirling, crashing minutes.

* * * * * *

Each side had the other pinned down. The NKPAs had us stopped, strung out in an exposed, enfiladed salient, firing at us from behind their stronghold cover. The Company Rocket Section came forward and fired a salvo against their bunker, which overhung our cover. The rockets blasted off and burst on the target. The bunker took the punishment; the NKPAs kept shooting at us.

My own Platoon survivors had closed with me. I found cover from direct fire behind a small bunker. Wounded Marines walked and limped past toward the rear, several pumping blood. Blood from one of them squirted and graffitied my helmet and face as he staggered past. The gore attracted the sympathy of a medical corpsman. I shouted that I wasn't hit, and pointed to another Marine down and bleeding. The corpsman ran to the collapsed Marine as NKPA bullets cracked and dirt spouted.

The sun had gone down behind further ridges. Firing continued as Reed and I tried to select the least suicidal of

"Half the platoon fell."

our action choices. He summarized in a carefully measured and controlled voice. "I've lost too many of my men! Two of my squad leaders are down! I can't go at them again!" I blurted, "I don't know what I've got left! If you can't make it, I can't make it! I don't have the troops! We'll be fighting in the dark if we go now!" Reed went over our options. "We can hold on. I think we can hold on, or we can pull back to the top and get air and artillery in the morning, when we can see what we're doing. I think we should hold. What do you say?"

The ridge spine down from the 854 ridge top had been a killing ground. I did not want to slink back up there and have to attack down over it again. Anyway, I didn't know how to conduct a withdrawal; Marine battle drill never included withdrawals. Our Company Commander's death had shaken us all, draining something from our cohesion and confidence. The march and climb and bloody assault had wrung out and battered us all; but the troops were still full of fight. None of us meant to pay the same butcher's bill twice. The Executive Officer, now Company Commander and in charge, joined the discussion. He supported our choice of "options." We stayed put.

The 76-millimeter had ended its shoot and been man-handled back to ground somewhere. We dug foxholes and crouched into them as it grew darker and colder. Machine gunners sited their weapons forward, our mortars registered defensive fires; we braced for the NKPA counterattack which would come in the darkest hours.

Marines who took to foxholes and bunkers dug by the run-away ROK soldiers discovered new revulsions. ROKs dug duplex foxholes; they threw their dead into the lower level, sprinkled dirt over them and used the upper level for protection and firing. Marines taking over and deepening the foxholes shoveled up the corpses' organs and limbs and chunks of rotten meat. The ROKs had used their bunkers as latrines. New occupants making emergency entrances sometimes sat or slid into their allies' sewage.

Starlight, crashing defensive mortar salvos, bursts of panic rifle fire and iron Manchurian cold made up the night. An NKPA reconnaisance probe onto the ridge top above us set off an exchange of fire; the probers ran off when the defenders proved alert and hostile. Deer moving up the slope near us made cracking and snapping noises, which NKPA scouts did not, setting off bursts of rifle and machine gun fire.

At dawn most of us dozed in our foxholes. In the favoring light I could make out the features of the meandering, intersected ridge top: natural parapets and hummocks plus defensive works that protected the NKPAs, from which they could shoot and throw grenades at us. One of them stuck his head up over his bunker for a look at us. His scowl made it clear neither surrender nor retreat was on his mind. Daylight grew, the troops woke up, took stock and began trading rifle fire with NKPAs.

The Company Commander ordered mine and yesterday's support Platoon to lead the restarted attack. Promised another air strike and an artillery barrage, we sorted ourselves out, reorganized and waited for the support.

At noon, a Marine air observer plane flew past to get us located, then flew a short distance out of the way. In minutes, a flight of F-51 fighter-bombers showing New Zealand insignia dove to eye level, strafing and napalming the NKPA stronghold. Machine gun bullets splintered trees and logs and spouted gravel. Napalm flames seared their targets. The New Zealanders' run-ins carried below the ridge tops from which they snapped into sharp climbs and chandelle circles, then dived again, firing into the stronghold. The NKPAs had learned in earlier battles how to engineer bunkers to frustrate air attacks.

As soon as the F-51s flew off, the artillery began its bombardment. The shells howled and crashed nonstop. Dust, smoke, debris, timbers and shell splinters leapt and tossed and flew as the orange bursts "walked" over the stronghold, the ground jolting and shuddering under the blasts.

The close-in crashing, concussing destruction made me a little manic.

"We're going to win! We're going to win this! Both squads close up here forward! Machine guns ready! Everybody move out when the WP shells hit!"

The bombardment ended with the pop of smoke shells. The white phosphorus cloud rolled over the target; we surged forward over the hook and into the NKPA stronghold.

My vision went black and white and two-dimensional again.

We fired and tossed grenades into bunker openings; we fired into bodies of the dead to make sure they were dead. An over-enthusiastic Marine machine gunner almost cut me down with a burst. A grenade tossed into a bunker seconds earlier blew another Marine flat as he fired into its entrance. My carbine jammed and went single shot, paying for a night scraping in foxhole gravel. NKPAs began scrambling out of bunkers to surrender, like rabbits flushed at our feet, holding surrender leaflets over their heads.

We advanced through the stronghold and held up at an embankment overlooking a cleared part of the ridge. Were any NKPAs left alive out there? A Marine was shot down, the fire sending us diving to cover. I chose a bomb crater. The artillery observer plane flew past again looking to get us located. To signal him, I armed a smoke grenade, ran forward, threw the grenade and ran back to my crater. If the air observer saw the smoke burst, so did the NKPA riflemen to our front. As I sat in the crater waiting for artillery fire, an NKPA fired, his bullet cracking into the dirt beside me. I assumed a near miss and a scare would satisfy him, and that he would take to cover. He didn't. His next bullet hit my cartridge belt, exploded one of the rounds and punched into my abdomen. I jackknifed and flopped over.

After the moment of impact and burning, I noticed the smoke from the exploded cartridge, the hole it had blown in my field jacket, other cartridges spilling out and the lack of bleeding or entrails. Two Marines jumped into the crater and tied a bandage around my waist.

I assumed I was shot through. "Am I bleeding from my back? "

"Naw." They secured the bandage and helped themselves to my weapon and bullets.

If I survived evacuation, all I had to worry about were internal punctures and bleeding and shock.

Stretcher-bearers dragged me out of the crater, supporting me as we started back over the ground we had attacked. As we picked our way through the wreckage and corpses, one of the bearers stepped on an NKPA box mine of the size that could have blown up yesterday's truck. His foot missed the firing hinge, or the mine wasn't armed. We stumbled on over it and up toward the ridge top, passing the Platoon Sergeant as he moved forward to take command of the Platoon.

I managed, "Good luck, Sergeant. It's all yours."

He answered, " Thank you, Lieutenant." I think he had other language in mind.

The three of us shuffled up over the ridge and down the trail toward the evacuation pad.

I had no sensation of ground covered or time passing.

Somewhere on the way down we came to a Marine guarding five POWs. One of the prisoners lay on the ground holding his midsection. The Marine shouted and motioned with his rifle for the prostrate POW to get up or else. The standing POWs pointed to their own stomachs gesturing as if something were passing through. Grimacing and grunting, the downed POW opened his blouse showing a mass of blood. Shot through the abdomen, he had walked a mile or more before he collapsed, hiding his wound. Wounded POWs are annoyances sometimes beyond their overstressed captors' patience.

Time and space drifted again until we arrived at the evacuation pad. The leader of the security squad I had detached to protect the pad sized up the state of my affairs.

"How bad, Lieutenant?"

"Not too," was my best.

"Good luck at medical."

"You guys all okay?"

"Yes, Sir. Thank you." I believe he really meant that "Thank you."

At my turn for treatment, the Navy doctor in charge asked, "What's your problem?"

"I got shot." I opened my jacket, pulled away the bandage and showed him the damage.

He took scissors from a pocket, cut a patch out of the shoulder of my field jacket and jabbed my arm with a blunt syringe of serum. Then he took forceps from another pocket and pulled an exposed shard of the bullet out of my abdomen. He handed me the piece of lead.

"Here. Show this to your grandchildren."

A corpsman took a band-aid—the home medicine cabinet type—and attached it over the wound. I wondered if this was the best they could do, or all they thought was needed, or that other treatment would be useless. Whatever they concluded, that ended the treatment.

A stretcher party arrived carrying another wounded Marine from my platoon. One of his stretcher bearers recounted what happened after the sniper leveled me and corpsmen led me to safety.

"The Third Platoon attacked the bunker that the NKPAs shot you from. But the goddamn NKPAs put shoe mines in front of it. This guy stepped on one. Sergeant Yellowhead led the charge into the bunker anyway and cleaned the NKPAs out. Took some prisoners. They couldn't tell which one shot you; there was only one rifle between them all. You know the guy shot before you? He died. Couldn't help him in time. Then some other guy got killed by our artillery. Don't we have enough trouble with the NKPAs? Goddamn!"

The "shoe mine" had blown off the stretchered Marine's right foot, the blast cauterizing the stump. The Marine had escaped the smashing injury to his crotch frequent in shoe mine wounds. He was alert and seemed in minimal pain, covered with the fine dust that high explosive blasts threw up, smiling almost awkwardly, as if he had stepped into a mess of some kind. Corpsmen gave him anti-tetanus and morphine shots, bandaged his curiously polished looking leg stump ever so carefully, packed him into the outrigged gondola on the next helicopter which clattered him away to the field hospital.

The last twelve hours had blurred into black and white: the marshaling and waiting to restart yesterday's stalled attack, the air strike this noon, the bombardment, the charge and the fight, the crack and punch of the sniper's 8 millimeter, Marines jumping into the line of fire dragging me to cover, stretcher-bearers leading me numbed and stumbling away from the fight, back up the ridge then down its fifteen hundred foot reverse scarp, step-by-step, punchy, here to the helicopter pick-up.

Within minutes another helicopter closed on the strip, hovered and began settling.

"Get on the stretcher, Lieutenant! Here's your ride!"

The corpsman shouted and dropped a stretcher at my feet, the medical helicopter closing, clattering above us, drafting dust, swiveling and settling onto its landing marker. I dropped down onto the stretcher. The corpsmen strapped me down, grabbed the stretcher up and lunged through flying dirt to the gondola, threw the gondola cover open, lifted and centered me and the stretcher securely, shouted, "Good luck," closed and latched the cover. I felt the helicopter lurch upward, then rock forward, bouncing and shaking, airborne again in seconds.

Would this clattering rattletrap stay airborne and deliver me to medical care? What about the pilot? Maybe he's a hot-dog who shows off in his newfangled contraption dicing past treetops and cliff sides? Did he know the route back to the Medical Company, or would he U-turn somewhere in the jumble of ridges and mountains and canyons, flying us, unsuspecting, back into North Korean antiaircraft fire?

Evacuation helicopters carried wounded in outrigged gondolas; one on each side holding a stretchered casualty. The gondola had the shape of a coffin. A small window in its cover deferred to the passenger's state of pain and agitation; it allowed him, strapped and boxed, to look upward and out during the flight and watch the rotor whirling. Seeing something moving and hearing something clattering reassured him that he wasn't actually in his coffin, already dead.

The helicopter lifted higher, then accelerated downward into a canyon, using the ridge tops as a screen. The defilade flight path took away the North Korean gunners' entertainment of tracking and shooting at the unprotected targets, or of tallying Marine casualties.

Bully for the gondola designer and his window with its rotor hub view! The sun rays shone on its right side; the pilot had pointed the flight path South, away from the enemy! After some minutes the helicopter slowed to a hover and touched down at what I hoped would be the Battalion Medical Company. The gondola cover flipped open and two corpsmen looked down through swirling dust to see what was left of the new arrival. Both grabbed stretcher handles, lifted it and me out of the gondola and hustled out from under the rotor's beheading radius.

The corpsmen carried me through a tent jammed with treated casualties to the examining room surgical table. Two Navy doctors opened my field jacket, tore away the bandage covering the wound and looked over the damage.

"What hit you?"

"A bullet."

"Not a mine or grenade splinter? A mortar shell piece?"

"No. A bullet."

"So I see. Doesn't look too bad. I've got to de-debris it. We can't leave any cloth or wood or gravel in it, or it will get septic."

The doctor started poking into popped-out muscle tissue with what looked like a dentist's pick. Watching him probe into my punctured tissue made it more painful. I tried to writhe away.

"Yes. I know. But this has to be clean of anything but lead. Lead bullets are sterilized when they hit and won't rot or rust. Bullet wounds self-cauterize; we can leave them alone."

The doctor stopped picking, and I stopped writhing. He applied a stethoscope to my abdomen.

"Good bowel sounds. Very good bowel sounds. No puncture. Peritoneum must be okay, too. You're in luck." He stuck a new band-aid over the wound.

"Okay to get up. Go to the corpsmen's station and tell them to give you some penicillin. They'll send you to the sleeping tent for the night; there will be corpsmen at the sleeping tent if this gives you trouble. Good luck. Get some sleep. I'll see you tomorrow. Did the corpsmen at evacuation give you a shot?"

"Yes."

"Did they say what it was, antibiotic or tetanus?"

"I don't remember."

"Tell the corpsman to give you a tetanus booster, too."

"Okay."

The doctor delivered the last instruction over his shoulder as he moved to attend the next casualty. The operating table had the dimensions of a saloon bar. I sat up and slid off, passing another Marine laid out at its opposite end. The fine dust from a close high-explosive blast covered his dungarees and face; his complexion had gone almost olive color, his dungarees smelled of TNT gas. Wherever the shell splinters had taken him, he'd been whacked too hard to pull through.

I lurched out into the dark, drifting between tent rows, looking for the corpsmen's tent and the tetanus and penicillin fixes. The minor wound, not a mutilation sending me hobbling or wheelchaired or stretchered back to the States, had gotten me out of enemy gun sights and away from his minefields for a few days.

Officer Candidate School instructors had solemnly warned all of us being readied to assault Japan in 1945 that accepting Marine Corps commissions as second lieutenants made us one of the Corps' two most expendable items: tent pegs and second lieutenants. The assault tactics taught us by the Marine Corps schools called for small unit leaders to charge ahead of the troops they commanded. As highly as we prized the commissions we trained for, the rank of second lieutenant seemed to be held in universally low esteem by higher commissioned ranks and experienced noncommissioned officers. Reports coming to us from the fights for Iwo Jima and Okinawa told of friends and classmates, also second lieutenants, already killed in action.

We told ourselves that it wouldn't happen to us. None of us resembled tent pegs. If we were correct in the second, we were dead wrong in the first. We discovered later that, as we received our commissions, we had been designated replacement Platoon commanders. We would have been fed into the six Marine Divisions after they landed on the Japanese home island of Kyushu. Ashore, the Allied landing force would have faced Japanese forces which outnumbered the American landing forces three to two.

Between wars I had joined the Reserves and been promoted to first lieutenant. I had been recalled into this war along with other reserve officers. The promotion in rank hadn't appeased or impressed the North Korean marksman who may have paid with his life for dropping me, with an undercharged cartridge at that. Anyway, the incident put QED on the Officer Candidate School verity, extended to include first lieutenants.

7
Medical Company

NORTH KOREA
SEPTEMBER 21–28 1951

The corpsman on duty greeted his new customer.

"How goes it, Lieutenant?"

"The doctor told me to ask for penicillin. I've got a bullet in the stomach."

"If you're walking, you're in luck. Drop your pants and skivvies."

I followed his instructions while he loaded a syringe and postured himself *en guarde* for the thrust.

He coaxed. "You've got to relax, Lieutenant. This has to go intramuscular or it won't work. It stings a little."

My pants and underpants "at half mast," he slapped one gluteal cheek and rapiered the syringe/ice pick into the other. The blunt needle rasped the muscle tissue and the penicillin burned like a bee sting.

"There. I'll see you again in the morning."

I forgot to ask for tetanus. "Where can I get something to eat?"

"The mess kitchen is closed, but there might be something there you can pick up. It's around to the right about fifty yards."

"Where's the sleeping tent?"

"Twenty yards or so past the mess tent. Go to the first, and you can't miss the second."

I pulled up my pants, walked out into the dark and turned right. I saw a lighted tent at the predicted fifty yards, the mess tent without the mess cooks. Cases of canned food looked appetizing but were sealed; walk-in refrigerators and freezers were all padlocked. I found a box of apples open and unguarded; apples it was—my breakfast, lunch and dinner. I helped myself and wolfed two or three, and walked back out into the dark, looking for the sleeping tent. I found it by following the sound of voices; it was full of casualties in the first two medical triages; the diagnosed fatally wounded had been sequestered elsewhere.

The cot nearest the entrance held Henry Rawlins, a Marine from my Platoon, one of my charges. He had been in the helicopter flight ahead of mine. A "shoe mine" victim, covered with explosion dust and smelling of TNT, his right pants leg had been scissored away and his right foot and lower leg had been amputated. Still partly anesthetized and badly wounded, he wanted to talk.

"How are you doing, Lieutenant?"

"How are *you* doing? Are you able to talk? When did you get hit?"

"Right after you did. There were mines in front of that bunker they shot you from. One of the mines got me. Are you okay?"

"Yes. Okay. Anyone else hit?"

"Wilson was killed by our own artillery. Jesus!"

Rawlins was tiring and drifting out of it.

"Why don't I write your family and tell them you'll be coming home? Give me the address, and I'll write a letter for you."

U.S. breweries enclosed stationery in each case of beer sold to troops in the field. Red-bordered Budweiser sheets with envelopes appeared from somewhere, and I addressed a note to Rawlins' mother in Belleville, Illinois.

9/21/51

Dear Mrs. Rawlins,

I am writing from the Third Battalion Medical Company where your son and I are wounded. He has had his right foot amputated but has no other injuries. He is talking to me as I write. The medical doctors say they expect a full recovery. He will be taken from here to a hospital ship until he can be flown to the United States. I cannot give the date for his departure from Japan or his arrival in the United States. He is in good spirits and sends you his best and asks that you not worry. He will write to you as soon as he is able.

Sincerely,
Lt. John Harper USMCR

I sealed it and wondered where to find the mail drop. Corpsmen carried in another casualty. Rawlins' crotch had escaped the "shoe mine" blast; this casualty's had not. His left foot had been amputated, and his crotch was heavily bandaged. The bandages configured to all the parts that should be there; something had been salvaged. Heavily anesthetized, he began moaning as if he remembered the blast and the wounding. He was beyond a letter home if I had known his address, and I was not up to composing a vague, understated note.

Across the tent another casualty stood up from his cot; splinter wounds and bandages over his entire front and side. Unable to tolerate partial clothing, he stood naked and shivering. I looked more closely at the drained face; he was Corporal Jack Peters, Company clerk. During the fight the day before, we in the assault Platoons were forward of and down the slope from the headquarters people.

While we were getting ourselves machine gunned, the Company Headquarters staff had taken direct fire from the North Korean field gun. The enemy had spotted and fired into the headquarters Marines on the ridge top for as long as they had artillery shells. Peters was one of the many wounded in the bombardment. I crossed the tent, got him to sit down, and called a corpsman's attention to his discomfort. Peters seemed unable to speak. He had been a bright and more than competent clerk, too old and savvy to be a corporal by choice. I didn't understand the term at the time, but he had to have been an alcoholic; always one of the few drunk after a beer ration.

Another casualty called for help through his anesthesia. A corpsman broke off record keeping and attended to what the patient needed.

I picked an unused cot and stretched out, waiting for something. I didn't know what I was waiting for. I didn't care what I was waiting for. I had both arms, both legs, both eyes and intact genitalia. I was neither cut up, shot up, dismembered nor disemboweled. I felt wrung out and drained and wired, and very lucky.

A Navy medical officer, a full commander, opened the tent flap and began his rounds, checking each of the twenty-some casualties. He saw my rank and apparent state of health and mobility.

"I'm Commander Burton. How goes it, Lieutenant?"

"Lieutenant Harper, Commander. Well enough, considering."

We shook hands, and he invited me to recuperate in the medical officers' quarters. I accepted and followed him to the doctors' tent.

"Sorry we only have a stretcher for you tonight. We'll get you a cot in the morning." The other doctors introduced themselves. A light rain had started. I thought about the comrades up on the hill, wet and hungry and under fire. I was given a blanket and lay down on the stretcher—and went out cold.

The doctors were up and out on their rounds at dawn. The Medical Company camp had been sited in a grove of trees near a riverbank. The river, at its dry season low, splashed and gurgled the way a river should, passing a place of mending. A spectacular bluff, topped with woods in fall colors, walled the far bank. Pleasing to look at under other circumstances, now it could be an approach route for guerrillas to surprise and take the near-defenseless camp under fire.

Mess cooks served a breakfast feast: fried eggs, bacon, bread and margarine and jam, all the delicacies I could eat, my first sit-down meal in weeks.

After dropping my pants for the corpsman's ice-picking and bee venom, I limped back to the doctors' quarters favoring my punctured, stinging backside. One of the doctors gave me a razor, soap and pointed the way to the officers' outdoor lavatory. The facility included a tree, a can of water, a mirror and a crude stand holding the predictable inverted

steel helmet basin. I cleaned up and went to the designated
MD for a wound inspection.

"The bullet hole is leaking a little but looking good, and
the bowel sounds are good, too. Have you had your penicillin?"

I answered that I goddamn well had and got a big laugh.
He applied a fresh band aid to the wound. "What happened to your hand?"

"I don't remember." The back of my left hand showed a
four inch slash I had picked up somewhere.

"Doesn't look too bad. The penicillin should take care of
it. Let us know if it doesn't. Where are you from,
Lieutenant?"

"Near Chicago."

"There's a coincidence. Chicago is where the medical
people learned how to treat—or not to treat—bullet wounds.
In the 1920s Al Capone and his friends sent so many riddled
competitors to hospitals that doctors decided to try out new,
less damaging treatment on his targets. Instead of mining
for the lead in the victims, they learned about leaving bullets
in place instead of gouging them out. The technique
worked, and we still use it. How about that?"

"Yeah."

Now, what to do? Better write to the home folks. The
Department of Defense will be on the job, and the home
front will get the "We regret to inform you . . ." pro forma
telegram that would conjure visions of disfigurement and
dismemberment and helplessness, transporting any next of
kin into panic. I located more of Budweiser's Bond and
turned out a long letter. Then the combination of North
Korean marksmanship and too much breakfast caught up
with me.

Cramps far more painful than the wounding itself seized
my insides. I lurched back to the MD's tent grunting and
pointing to my midsection. The doctor diagnosed the problem. The undercharged bullet hadn't punctured the peri-

toneum or the intestine. Its punch had "bruised" the intestine, making it intolerant of the morning's wonderful load of fried food and other treats; too much breakfast too soon. He gave me a fix of belladonna pills that replaced the pain with euphoria, a "trip." I went back to my stretcher in the doctors' quarters and drifted into a nap.

Dinner included fresh meat and vegetables—more country club living and country club cuisine—with a war just up the road. The nearest artillery batteries were two miles north. They had been thumping enthusiastically during the afternoon; now their firing stopped. The cease-fire not being followed by a crush of retreating vehicles and troops on the supply route meant the North Koreans had been dealt more of their desserts, not that the front had caved in and the guns overrun in a bug-out retreat.

River sounds and the hum of the camp generator were the only noises. More letters to write under a genuine, wired electric light, then dreamless sleep.

The next morning, Commander Burton noticed a blood stain, not of my making, on my cot/stretcher.

"Take that thing away and burn it. I won't have blood-stained equipment used here. Get the lieutenant a cot or a new stretcher."

Room service went into action and a new cot appeared. I had just been guaranteed another day and night of Five Star comfort.

After breakfast, the morning ice-picking and a fresh band-aid, I visited the sleeping ward tent to inquire after new arrivals. Peters and Rawlins and the other badly wounded Marine had been sent toward Japan. A new casualty, Kucic, had arrived. He had been hit in the back with a stick-mine fragment. It had been extracted and the wound closed. Kucic was in high spirits.

"Looks like I'm on my way home, Lieutenant! How about you?"

"I think I'll stick around now that the shooting's stopped. How did the Platoon do?"

"Well, we got the two 'killed in actions.' We got those two crackups the first week. We got those two guys shot in the legs last week." He gave a knowing look. The two leg "casualties" had to have been planned reciprocal woundings. "Sergeant Henry was shot through the knee. He didn't seem too bad off, though; not much bleeding. He's damn lucky if he gets away with that one." We went through the names of thirteen others plus the two mine casualties. "The Platoon should be down to 20 out of 44."

"That's what I count, too." Fifty-five percent casualties; not as bad as the late, great World War II, but impressive when the casualties were my charges.

"Did Captain Henderson leave a family?"

"Yes, he did. A wife and two daughters."

"That's too bad. He was a good officer. We all liked him."

"Can I do anything for you while you're here? If I can, let me know. I'm bunking with the doctors."

"Sounds soft, Lieutenant."

"It is that." We shook hands.

I walked to the records tent to inquire after the next-of-kin addresses of my two "killed in actions." I wrote what turned out to be appropriate sentiments. Both families later acknowledged my letters with thanks.

Rumor had it that a commercial cable telegraph company had opened for business nearby. A short walk down a dirt road, and there it stood: Nipon Cable Service. Operating in an elegant cut lumber shack, wires strung up through a hole in the roof to trunk lines hanging from tree branches; all high-tech and open for business. I composed a brief, upbeat message addressed to Barrington, Illinois, light years away somewhere to the east. I paid for it in South Korean won that I had kept through it all. I met a corporal from the Company sending his own message. He had taken his second wound, and it would send him home. He had been reserved and almost hostile in dealing with officers during training. Now, his manner had changed, because the pressure of authority was removed or because he had seen officers getting shot up, or both.

"You're out of it, Corporal. Don't spend it all in Japan."

"Not about to, Lieutenant. The geishas can get it from someone else. I never want to see this part of the world again. I'm on my way."

We walked back toward the Medical Company comparing views on the fight.

"Who was responsible for that slaughter?"

I thought the Battalion had gotten off lightly. We had only under-equipped North Koreans to contend with. The Regiment on our left had collided with a hardened Chinese Communist Forces Division and paid heavily for it.

"The Fifth Regiment ran into the Chinese. They really had a fight."

"I was thinking more of the Seventh. Those guys were whipped when we relieved them last week—or was it last month?"

"The Seventh took on more than it could handle. That hill, 1052, is too much for one Regiment; too much ground and too many North Koreans. More of us should have been put into the act." We traded opinions and casualty names until we separated. I assumed he went to Japan and then the States; we never met again. Breakfast began exploding in my bruised intestine; I headed for my fix of belladonna, and spent the rest of another day zonked.

Without assignments or responsibilities for the first time in six months, I ate and slept and loafed; a prisoner-at-large with every privilege and creature comfort, ordered to stay put under medical care. Although the artillery to the north stayed quiet, the war hung too close and too recent. I wrote more letters.

"The fight must have stopped," Commander Burton announced at dinner. "The last flight of wounded includes the first new VD cases." VD cases showing up in a forward Battalion Aid Station were hard evidence of something resembling a cease-fire in North Korea. The troops had found something more intriguing to do than shoot at the North Koreans.

"The area has been swept of civilians; they're all in internment camps. The villages and food stocks have all been burned. Where do the guys find the broads?" A junior doctor was appalled.

"In caves. Just like the limerick. 'There was a young fellow named Dave . . .' "

"These cases don't even respond to penicillin! The women must be in terrible shape! Who wants them?"

" 'C'est la guerre.' That means war makes its own rules. That's not an original notion. I heard it somewhere."

I looked in at the casualty sleeping tent to see if any new wounded were from my Company. They were not, but three of the new arrivals had a rough ride back. During their evacuation by ambulance-jeep an alert North Korean mortar crew observed their sortie, or their departure was exquisitely mistimed. A mortar salvo "bracketed" the road and the jeep. The shells missed the jeep and the splinters missed the riders. The driver panicked, accelerated too fast into a turn and rolled the jeep. The three wounded stayed strapped in and roll bars resisted the impact. Shaken and irritated but not re-injured, they made it clear they didn't need the gratuitous thrills, and they wanted a meeting with the nervous jeep driver.

*   *   *   *   *   *

The comfortable seven-day "weekend" at Medical Company's "Riverside Country Club" ended when I decided the war couldn't get on without me (and the Navy doctors declared me whole again and fit for duty). I rejoined my Company, wearing a fresh band aid, on the ridge we—they— had captured. We occupied the ridge until relieved by another Marine Battalion five weeks later. I needed to talk very fast to explain pulling out of a fight half won and taking a week's medical leave with only a band-aid wound as evidence of medical need

The Company and the Regiment stayed on the front until November. We were replaced and rotated into reserve a mile to the rear for rest, replacements and training. The rest camp had been sited between a river and a high ridge which paralleled the front; the ridge shielding the camp from enemy observation and most of his artillery. We lived in tents, ate cooked food, and slept secure and warm at night. We were also prepared to mobilize and move forward, to the flanks, even to the rear, on hours' notice. The one-mile interval between the front and the reserve camp made the difference between creature comforts and nominal safety, and none of either. It was a time to get ourselves back together, size up newcomer replacements, acquire minor luxuries, and send reliable agents to Japan to procure hard liquor for whoever had a thirst.

*　　*　　*　　*　　*　　*

In late November, the Battalion held a memorial service for the Marines killed in the September and October fighting. The service was held nearby on a riverbank, a wide graveled stretch left by the low water. We assembled and were given programs containing a short prayer and the names of the Battalion's twenty-one dead.

A battery of artillery and its camp were sited five hundred yards down the river from us; its six howitzers dug in on the opposite bank The howitzers muzzle flashes reached only the gravel banks and open water on their side. They could fire over our heads without starting fires, deafening us or blowing our tents away. As the chaplain began the service, the artillery began firing. It was less a distraction than an accompaniment to the memorial. The twenty-one dead had been our friends, comrades and troops for whom we had been responsible. The program listed our Company Commander, a fine Marine and leader. The names from my platoon included a rifleman blown up by shell fire and another killed by rifle fire. Always present and overriding was the old troopers' saw, "There, but for the grace of God. . . . " The firing and the service continued.

Miles to the north, a fed-up enemy began retaliating with return fire. Without ranging shots, he opened a sustained, observed, counter-battery bombardment, sending shell after shell howling over our heads and crashing into the artillery camp. High explosive flashed and roared, debris flew, fires started and flared out of control, black smoke thermaled. Troops scampered for cover, and vehicles raced to get away from the camp, now a target. Whenever the fall of the shells drifted away from the camp, line-crosser observers hidden on overlooking ridge tops radioed corrections to redirect the fire back onto the camp. Genuine as our feelings were for our dead comrades, we found great diversion watching a comfortable, rear-echelon unit lose its collective nerves and have its amenities burned and blown to bits.

Unhurried by the enemy shells rushing overhead or the blasts and destruction across the river, the memorial service continued and concluded on schedule. The artillery duel stopped. The mess sergeant served supper on time.

*   *   *   *   *   *

The bodies of the dead we had honored became the responsibility of 1st. Lt. Charles Reynolds USMCR, Graves Registration Officer for the First Marine Division. Charlie's staff took charge of the corpses, verified identities, notified the Department of Defense, bagged the remains and shipped them back to the States.

His staff operated the ice machine whose product chilled and preserved the cadavers. For us, the living, the same machine made the ice that chilled the mixed drinks for the

Battalion Officers' Club. We routinely plunked Charlie's ice into our bourbon-and-Cokes without a thought of its official, or possibly its recent, use. If we hinted that it contributed an unusual flavor to our drinks, Charlie suggested changing brands of bourbon and upgrade from the one-dollar stuff to the two-dollar stuff.

Charlie, The Merry Mortician, made himself welcome everywhere in the Division. "Just get us the ice, Charlie!" If you could joke and drink with him, you didn't need his official services, and your luck was holding.

*   *   *   *   *   *

I did not encounter any of the Medical Company doctors again. I met Kucic, the Marine who had taken the mine splinter in his back, on the street in Chicago a year or two later. He drove a taxi for a living, so much troubled by the wound he said he needed a less physical occupation. His only affordable source of medical treatment, the Veterans Administration Hospital, wouldn't take an interest in his condition. I had neither advice nor a job to offer him.

Another of the mine casualties visited my father before I returned home. On his way home, the Marine made a courtesy call bringing Father "the news from the front." The two had traded war stories, the amputee glad to be alive and in the best of spirits. A decorated veteran of three wars, Father was deeply moved by the young Marine on crutches, an empty pants leg hanging, a land mine having taken his leg.

War had changed since Father had "answered the bugles' call." The frequent weapon in the new wars, land mines, are cheap and indiscriminate. Not designed to smash and riddle and kill, they wait to mutilate and hospitalize. Father mentioned the amputee's visit only once, in a letter. I assume he compared the Marine's luck with mine—and his own. I never asked if the Marine had left his address.

8

Under Fire

What Korea Was Really Like

by Lt. John W. Harper, USMCR

From the LIFE *issue of December 3, 1951*

During what was officially described as a quiet period on the Korean battle front, John W. Harper, a Marine lieutenant in a line company, wrote this letter to his father, a Marine lieutenant-colonel in World War II. It was not intended for publication, but LIFE *was given permission to publish it, unedited, as a small masterpiece of reporting on life in the front lines at a time when nothing was supposed to be happening. (*LIFE *Ed.)*

October 14, 1951

Dear Paw,

Please excuse the delay in writing. It was not caused by anything more serious than natural laziness and inconvenience. I regained the 3rd Battalion on October 1. I discovered that H Company had been assigned a sector on the battalion left which extends down to the base of the hill and into a valley. My Platoon Sergeant had taken over the platoon after I was hit and carried it right on through to the conclusion of the assault and then set it up in a very good defensive position. He did a fine job then, in fact from the time I took over the platoon, and I have recommended him for a meritorious promotion to the next higher grade, although he has only been a sergeant for about five months. I also discovered that one of the squad leaders, Sergeant Yellowhead, conducted a one-man banzai charge during the assault, killing a number of gooks and collecting four or five

prisoners. For this, he was recommended for the Bronze Star
Medal by the other platoon leader present. After getting back to
the company, I found a new C.O. The former exec had been sent
to Regt. having served four months on line, and also the second
lieutenant in charge of the 2nd platoon, having been five months
on line, had been given a job at battalion. The 60-mm mortar
officer, too, was rotated rearward to the 4.2 mortars, leaving three
vacancies. Then the 1st platoon commander was given an emergency leave home.

I ended up with the 60-mm mortar section in the company.
The other day we caught four gooks cooking rice outside their
bunker.[1] I decided to try the new toys on their breakfasting.
I won't say that we splashed mortar shells right into their cook
bowls, but all four were in a state of collapse when we ceased
firing.

To go back to when I first got back to the line, the minute
I arrived I could tell that morale was fair. From a quarter of a
mile back, I could hear whooping, laughing, cursing, trees being
felled, holes being dug, trails being hacked out, word of one kind
or another being passed up and down the line from bunker to
bunker with yells the gooks across the way could surely hear and
probably understood. The troops all had unnecessarily big grins
for me when I trooped the platoon line to see how they were set
in. Light wounds remain a big joke and excellent luck, it seems,
especially for rank of any kind.

---

[1] This is one of the most vivid images I recall. The name "Korea" translates
to Land of the Morning Calm. After dark, the night humidity slides down
the ridge sides into the valleys and cools, filling them with mist almost to
the ridge tops. After a still, clear night, the first morning hour remains still
and clear. In the "morning calm" this day, the crest of a lower ridge facing
us stood above the mist line. On it an NKPA bunker faced us at a range of
about a thousand yards. I could see several NKPA soldiers carelessly, impu-
dently lounging or cooking near the bunker. One of the loungers reclined,
smoking a cigarette. As he raised and lowered his cigarette, inhaling and
exhaling, the tobacco smoke hung about his face and head, the morning air
so still it did not draft the smoke away. I suppose his enjoying himself and
his insouciance and apparent contempt for us made me determined to
blow him to bits. As I admitted, I was never sure that I got the job done.
(5/18/01)

That night was the last of the very active nights as far as infiltrators were concerned. The whole company line is interconnected with telephones so that the nightly frights and jitters can be communicated from one end of the line to the other with maximum speed. As soon as darkness settles there is a wait of about a half an hour before the first man gets rattled and heaves the first grenade. Then someone else hears the bushes shake and heaves two or three, then he gets to a phone and wants a flare so he can see the charging hordes. If a parachute flare is shot over his head, the hard white light of the burning magnesium hanging from the falling and drifting parachute throws jet black shadows through the trees. The shadows move, creep and jump from side to side just like a gook. The only satisfaction they give is that they fail to reveal the imagined charging phalanx. One night on the platoon phone watch went something like this when my Platoon Sergeant was on the phone.

(Crash of a grenade)

Plt. Sgt.: Who threw that last grenade, that you first squad?
Phone (whispered trembling voice): Yea! There's something in the wire!

(Crash of a second grenade)

Plt. Sgt.: Did you get him? You better have!
Phone: Yea! I heard his pants rip on the wire!
Plt. Sgt.: Never mind pantsing him. Did you kill him? (Wild confusion on the other end of the line followed by another grenade crash)
Plt. Sgt.: OK! 60-mm fire coming up.

(A delay of five or ten minutes while the mortar crew is woken up, gotten to the gun and the rounds pooped out. They crash into the hillside close to our lines.)

Plt. Sgt.: How does that look to you?
Phone: Fine! Fine! Only now it sounds like somebody chokin' a pheasant!!

Plt. Sgt.: Choking a pheasant! How do you know? Go back to sleep!
Phone: OK, OK. Thanks for the mortar fire.

(Half an hour passes)

Phone: Platoon CP!! Platoon CP! Cee Pee!!
Plt. Sgt.: Yea?
Phone: They're blowin' a bugle!!
Plt. Sgt.: Oh? Well? What are they playing?
Phone: I dunno. I can't make it out. I tell you they're blowin' bugles!!
Plt. Sgt.: Who's blowing bugles?
Phone: The gooks!!
Plt. Sgt.: How far away are they? Can you tell?
Phone: I guess about across the valley on the other side of the ridge. (Fully nine hundred yards)
Plt. Sgt.: Well can't you tell what tune they're playing? Listen close and see if it's on the hit parade.
Phone (squawks and rattling noises, then very calmly): I don't know what they're playing. All I know is they're blowin' a bugle.
Plt. Sgt. : Roger. OK. But if you hear a piano and violin, let us know and we'll come and help you get back to the rear.
Phone: Yes, Sgt. (Followed by sputtering noises)

Later on, one of the troops heard noises in front of him and screamed for a parachute flare. When he got it, he could see the squirrels making the noise. In another hole, having heard a noise, a rifleman prepared to toss a grenade and roused his buddy in doing so. As he wound up to make the throw the buddy sat up and the grenadier smacked the grenade into the buddy's teeth, knocking him cold. This threw his aim off, and the grenade flew out, hit a tree, bounced back and exploded just a few feet from the bunker. The grenadier thought that a gook had tossed it back at him, so he threw another half dozen grenades in all directions to defend himself. When his panic subsided, he realized what had happened and helped his buddy look for his teeth in the dark.

Yesterday the 7th Marines on our left, under orders from X Corps, had to run a combat patrol (pronounced Probing Attack by the press, I believe) onto the ridge to our front. They trundled up fourteen (sic) tanks, ran an air strike, and fired artillery and mortars, mine included, in battery and battalion salvoes all morning and early afternoon. In mid-afternoon the patrol moved through our lines and minefield and on out into the wide open valley.

From my own OP, I had a fifty-yard-line seat of the whole show just like a football game, only the other team not only fought our team, but they shot at the spectators as well.[2] The infantry was preceded by the tanks which drew fire from a 76-mm up on a high ridge about two miles to the front. The long rounds from the 76-mm landed all around my bunker because the tanks thoughtfully parked right to my front.

The first round hit three men in the 3rd platoon to my right. Another, a dud, missed the new company commander by about four feet. Another cut my telephone line to the mortars, in effect putting them out of the fight because I couldn't shift their fire as the infantry advanced. So we watched. The tanks took up positions out in the open and began to whack away with their 90-mm at point blank range, about six hundred yards, at the little ridge. The 76 gun put round after round within yards of them. But they nonchalantly stood their ground firing 90s and machine guns whenever the infantry radioed for it.

I finally spotted the 76 by its peculiar muzzle blast. It took about ten seconds for the rounds to hit after being fired, ten

---

[2] A peculiarity of combat is that the troops in a fight see little of their fight. Their concentration is on the narrow part of the field to their immediate front, the source of greatest danger. This day, I could take in the whole panorama of the fight along several thousand yards of the enemy front: the air strikes, the supporting Marine tanks, the fall of my own and our heavier supporting mortar and artillery barrages, the North Korean defensive mortar and artillery fire and the fall of their shot and explosives into our lines, and the movements of the attacking Marines and of the defending North Korean troops.

The official 1st Division report of this action describes it as a much bloodier fight than I realized as I watched. The same report dates it as taking place 16 October, a date inconsistent with the date of my letter. I may have written my letter in pieces several days apart, dating only page one. We rarely knew the days or dates. If the Special Services sent us college football scores, it was probably Monday. If they sent professional scores, it was probably Tuesday. I never understood why we were expected to give a damn about who mauled whom in ballparks 8,000-10,000 miles to the east. (5/18/01)

"The flares drift."

seconds to ponder a misspent life and swear never to drink more
than three Martinis at a sitting again as long as-I-live *crash*.
Shooting at the tanks that time. Serves them right for moving out
in front of us *crash* . . . *s*peaking of Martinis, and so on, until the
infantry broke cover charging across the valley and up the ridge.
No sooner had they begun their dash when a gook 82-mm mortar
splashed a fountain of dust and smoke right at the feet of one of
them. A Navy Corpsman who must have nerves of steel and ice
water for blood, whoever he is, rushed to the fallen Marine, in
full view of the enemy, in an obviously zeroed-in spot, opened his
pack, pulled out his bandages and went to work. In a few minutes, someone coaxed a South Korean stretcher team out to pick
him (the casualty) up and carry him back.

Another 82 went to work on our lines, joining the 76. They
kept firing and we kept firing, both close support and counter
battery on the ridges and ravines of the big hill, 812, to the front.

The attack patrol regrouped under the little ridge to the front
and moved up onto it as rapidly as their equipment would per-
mit. They climbed to a level just under the skyline on our side
and moved quickly toward the known bunkers. The tanks by now
were blazing away, joined by a 75-mm recoilless (cannon) higher
up on our ridge. A gook popped out of one of the bunkers to see
how close the attackers were moving, and the 75-mm slammed
one right into him. Another trotted up from somewhere underground and took his place. When the patrol got to within about
seventy-five yards of the bunker position, he fired a shot with his
rifle and the patrol took cover. Round after round of 90-mm and
75 burst on and near the position. The ridge from the bunker on
up to the right was raked back and forth by tank and infantry
machine gun fire, plus 75 recoilless. But every time the patrol
tried to move, the little gook, clearly visible in his new green
quilted winter uniform, would pop up, fire a few rounds and
duck back underground before a fresh storm of TNT and steel
broke over his head.

For some reason, the gooks didn't drop mortars on the patrol
while it was on the ridge. All the fire seemed to fall on the spot
where its route crossed our lines. As the sun went down, the
patrol pulled back under cover of a heavy white phosphorus
smoke screen. Then all the gook fire shifted to our lines and rear.
They dropped a few within fifty feet of the 6o-mm section area,
but no one in the section was hurt. Aside from that, today was a
beautiful, quiet Indian summer day.

The surrender propaganda leaflets (enclosed) in another envelope are dropped impartially from airplanes, half to the gooks,
half for us. They seem to work. The company picks up one or two
(NKPA) deserters a day. One of my agents conned the Red bills
(communist money) off one of the deserters who said he had
been told that the Russian Army was coming through here any
day now. We also use a loudspeaker set up on a hillside to broad-
cast propaganda. It pulled twenty-eight (NKPA) deserters in two
nights. So much for the war news.

Thanks again for your fine services, and thanks to Carrie for
her "get well" note. The wound causes *no* inconvenience and is
closing nicely. I've been on a patrol (no shooting) and am doing
everything else I am supposed to do, and the wound causes no
trouble whatever. My rugby knee injury will cause me much more
grief in the future than the wound ever will.

Will write again much sooner.

Regards,

Your Son

9

First to Fight

NORTH KOREA

OCTOBER 1951

"Who's Company? Say again! The rumor says who?"

"Captain Frank Pelham. Who can handle it better?"

Captain Sam Potter had heard the rumor. Helicopters would airlift an infantry Company into the front line facing the North Korean Peoples Army. Frank Pelham's Company would put dash and elan into an operation that showcased Marine Corps style war making. Captain Frank Pelham, USMC, claimed his great grandfather to have been one Major John Pelham, Confederate States Army. The Marine Division's officer ranks, crowded with graduates of Virginia Military Institute and The Citadel, would be expecting success for the latter-day Confederate's coup.

"This war is in Korea! We're in Korea in 1951, not Virginia in 1863! Somebody tell them!" Captain Sam Potter, trying sarcasm to pull the Marine Division forward out of time warp, saw the maneuver as a logistic extravagance.

"We rebels don't care who we fight if they come from the goddamn North . . . Korea, China, Russia, Pennsylvania, Massachusetts . . . wherever." Captain "J" Peter Appleyard, a native of Union City, Tennessee, took any opening to remind comrades he came of rebel stock and from, by God, Tennessee. Potter enjoyed the comrades impugning the allegiance of the folks in the rebel's hometown.

"Which the hell side were they on?"

"Closet Yankees, that's what they were."

Potter knew that Appleyard had to take the hoots; the career Marine didn't want to face a superior, confessing he had bloodied himself restarting the Civil War. Appleyard had joined the Corps after working through a state college somewhere in Tennessee. Wars gave the Appleyards chances to practice their trade, to be recognized and to win awards and promotions. He had added the initial "J" to prefix his given name, thus creating his middle name; all the generals in the Marine Corps date-of-rank list had middle names.

Potter had been given his middle name at his christening in Darien, Connecticut. The Corps had been relentless in hunting down its Reserve officers and activating their commissions as the war continued. It reclaimed Potter from his family's bank. The Corps retrained him and sent him to Korea, assigning him duties removed from finance. He became a Regimental Intelligence Officer.

Potter maintained a distance from everyone; the Corps would not change his manner. Appleyard, the Operations Officer, stayed with his backwoods accent and mannerisms, paid attention to the business at hand. Potter gave him credit for his accomplishments, given what he had to work with. Appleyard's palaver and labored enunciation annoyed Potter. He would have preferred the uproar of shellfire to Appleyard's gravelly voice, reciting his stream of consciousness or talking his way through a motor or paperwork activity. Potter and his academic roommates had learned to respect one another's concentration.

Both reported to the Regimental Executive Officer, Chief of Staff Lieutenant Colonel Kluck. Potter enjoyed his superior's name, the same as that of an Imperial German General of clouded reputation, properly pronounced with a long "u." Anyone of inferior rank who addressed him using barnyard pronunciation received a homework lesson.

Potter admired his gift for tactics, managing and overseeing, and salesmanship. The way Potter saw it, Kluck didn't order operations, he gave presentations and sold them. Potter noticed that other subordinates stopped smiling at Kluck's name and physique after hearing him introduce an operations plan. At or near the Marine Corps' minimum height, refreshingly civilized and clear in his orders, Kluck drilled into both subordinates that wars were won by prepared troops massed in place in time; the enemy located, identified and counted, also in time. Kluck supervised as Appleyard did the first, Potter the second. Directing his two alien-to-each-other officers, Kluck and the Regiment kept winning its fights. Potter enjoyed working for the plain-talking winner, but he did not enjoy living within earshot of the drawling, gabby Confederate.

The colonel called a meeting with Appleyard and Potter. "This confirms the rumor. Division is sending Pelham and the Division Reconaissance Company up to the peak of Hill 884 to relieve the South Koreans there. They will go by air—helicopters. A front line relief by air will be a 'first' for the Division. They move out—fly out—tomorrow at noon. This will be Pelham's first direct adventure with the North Koreans. Pelham and his front will come under our command. We'll own him. He will not come under the Third Battalion. He reports to us direct. So we'll give him all support. Questions?"

"Colonel, has the artillery been told they will have more front to cover?" Appleyard playing at Regimental Commander.

"Yes. Pelham shanghaied his own forward observer. That must have been something of a fight in itself." Potter picked up the colonel's humor. Artillerymen enjoyed the security of infantry Regiments protecting their front. Potter visualized the artilleryman, strapped into a racketing helicopter, panicked and squeezed between grinning, unsympathetic infantrymen as he hurtled toward enemy guns.

Sensing the politics, Pelham's political muscle, in summoning officers from other echelons, Appleyard decided to test his own by volunteering Potter's skin.

"Colonel, maybe we should be getting firsthand intelligence on what's up there if we're going to own that part of the front."

"Captain Potter, what do you think?"

"I'll review what I have, which should be current, and advise the Colonel."

"Okay, that's it. Appleyard, make sure all your people understand *everything* at stake here...*everything*. They'll have real work to do on this."

"Yes, Sir, Colonel."

Appleyard had Potter cornered, identifying Potter's problems, suggesting how he solve them. If Potter had thought fast enough he might have volunteered to go up to

884. Now, he could not. He could have preempted
Appleyard by suggesting Appleyard reconnoiter the supply
routes to the peak—all the goddamn way to the top.
Appleyard's solution would have been to annex the same
coolies and the same trail networks the Korean Labor
Corps had been climbing for weeks. Potter had appreciated
the force opposite Pelham from order-of-battle data, its
numbers and weapons and readiness, and that a renegade
Japanese general commanded it. He didn't need a hike up
884 to extend his ken in the matter, and he would not con-
cede the round to Appleyard.

Later, Colonel Kluck sent a clerk to tell Potter to come to
his headquarters tent.

"Division sent me a message that the Battalion on the 7th
Korean right, near where Pelham is going in tomorrow, got
raided hard last night. The ROKs whom Pelham is relieving
may start showing signs they're pulling out by celebrating in
sight of the NKPAs. If they do, they'll sell out the relief. Get
everything you can from Division on the NKPA unit that did
the raid. I'll do the same from Xth Corps. Captain Potter, get
yourself up there *before* tonight for a look around. Do not
stay up there overnight. Do go back up tomorrow. Greet
Pelham warmly, in person, then come back and report."

The order delighted Potter. His colonel had just nullified
Appleyard's winning round.

"Yes, Sir." The colonel had not referred to the name or
function of the unit being flown up to 884; he identified it as
"Pelham." Confederate bloodlines got you further in the
Corps than a Princeton BA, so Potter learned early on, and
Appleyard's drawling reminded him.

Potter telephoned Division intelligence. Line-crossers
confirmed that the renegade Japanese general's Division
had made the probe which battered the ROK lines. Colonel
Kluck advised Potter that Xth Corps' intelligence confirmed
the other's. Pelham would be warned that the North Korean
Division and its soldier-of-fortune general must not be taken
as just another battered enemy unit.

Potter ordered his jeep and prepared for a night in the open; Appleyard was rousting and dragooning the supply people to prepare for the Division's favorite son.

That afternoon Potter climbed to the 884 peak, a vertical sixteen hundred goddamn feet. He found the ROK unit reveling at getting off the mountain.

Potter made several assumptions, each a threat. The Japanese general and his outposts could not miss this celebrating from across the valley, nor misjudge what set it off. The general may have already missed his chance to smash into the anarchy and congestion of a relief in progress. The fly-in relief would identify his new opponent as someone's "fair-haired," as Occidentals put it. The officer in command had to be someone's favorite, his unit selected to fly into position, spared ordinary foot-soldiers' labor of climbing to it. Bloodying this upstart's nose would serve notice who bossed this—his—sector. Potter knew the general would also recognize the Marine field dress, reminding him of the recent Pacific war and the Imperial Army's—his previous Army's—defeats at the hands of the U.S. Marines. It could be the general believed he had "face" to recoup and scores to settle.

Potter returned with his guesses to his jeep, radioed Colonel Kluck that he was *in situ*, ate a canned food supper and laid out his sleeping bag for a cold night. In the morning he again climbed goddamn 884 before Pelham clattered in to dismount from his Sikorsky charger. Potter almost expected Pelham to leap out, saber at the ready, wearing a plumed Confederate campaign hat instead of a camouflaged helmet. Pelham knew better. He had, however, indulged himself in a pair of carefully polished hunting boots.

Potter told him everything he knew that might unsettle him and congratulated him heartily on his bold master stroke. Then he left Pelham's dragoons to their mountain-top, swashbuckling and spoiling for a big fight.

On his descent back to his jeep, Potter visualized the reception Appleyard would get from the infuriatingly possessive, slowpoke supply people.

"I am delivering Colonel Kluck's orders, Major."

"Goddamn! I'll talk to the colonel about this—and about you. That will be all, Captain."

He could hear Appleyard reporting his reception to his colonel, who would get a prompt complaint from the supply people. The colonel would listen briefly, then break in explaining clearly how things goddamn were and how things goddamn were going to be.

Potter reviewed to himself what he'd seen of the ground on 884, his impression of Pelham's fly-in and deployment, and of Pelham's composure and grasp of what to do after he landed. He concluded so far so good for the cavalier.

At his desk, he returned a call from Division Intelligence. He got more disquieting news. The samurai facing Pelham, General Kobiyashi, drove his troops ruthlessly into attacking, regardless of losses. Pelham's front faced north; the north face of 884 presented a nearly unclimbable pitch to attackers. With or without Kobiyashi's tommy-gunners at their backs, Potter knew that fully loaded NKPA troops could climb and attack up mountainsides like bugs walking up walls. He would report the intelligence to Colonel Kluck, and Pelham would get orders to take extra security measures.

When Potter took his advice to his colonel, Kluck reported Pelham's "thank you," and said he would transmit the ominous intelligence soonest, grumbling about the Supply people and why Appleyard couldn't light a fire under them.

Potter returned to his office summarizing to himself, " . . . the round goes to Samuel Chase Potter—in fact, two rounds! But if Pelham gets whacked before he gets the support he needs, if the samurai pulls off a surprise, the round and the fight may go to the samurai, and we'll all swing for it. I'll propose more aerial surveillance."

Potter called Division, whose information included more menace. Within the hour Division had debriefed a line-crosser agent who reported that political officers were on Kobiyashi's case, and that unusual numbers of NKPA deserters were crossing the lines to surrender. The last item magnified the threat. Potter had been lectured that soldiers weighing desertion often took action to sneak away when told they would be ordered into an attack. Potter collected his notes and asked to see his colonel.

"Yes, I agree, Captain. I'll tell them I want new reconnaissance and photographs tomorrow. All they usually give us are pictures of woods and dirt roads and trails. But if the trees and brush have up and moved around since the last photographs, well...I think both you and Appleyard better go up to 884 tomorrow and make sure Pelham has his feet on the ground."

*   *   *   *   *   *

"J, the colonel wants us both to go up to visit Pelham tomorrow and make it clear to him that a real butcher is looking at him from across the valley. Are you up to it?" If he caught the sarcasm, Appleyard ignored it.

Appleyard riposted. "Sure I am. What did the ROKs leave Pelham in the way of defenses? Did you have time to look them over?"

"Flimsy bunkers, poorly camouflaged and poorly sited, the usual latrine discipline. It's all over the place. Division has to do more than give Pelham a cheering section. Pelham may impress Pelham, but he won't scare Kobiyashi."

"First light is 0630. We should leave here no later. The climb is 500 meters vertical and 700 horizontal. How long did you take yesterday?" Appleyard's earlier choice of, "Did you have time?" and now, "How long did it take you?" implied inattention or loitering by Potter.

"Two hours; the pitch isn't too bad." Returning Appleyard's tone, "We can take our time. Sortie headquarters here at 0630, and we'll close on Pelham at 0830 latest. I'll get Division's most recent before we move out. The colonel will give me his latest tonight."

"Maybe we should drive to the supply base tonight. Move up from there at 0630."

"I don't want to be cut off from Division's intelligence all night tonight. If Kobiyashi moves, it will be at night. If more agents or deserters come across, they'll do it at night. You go ahead if you want to. I'll join you at 0630. If something holds me up, go on up without me. I'll catch up or join you at Pelham's."

Appleyard had clearly made up his mind to go for broke. "I'll go on to the top tonight. I'll go tonight. You can join us at the top."

"It's your call." Potter saw that Appleyard had been caught up in the Pelham excitement. He wanted time alone with Pelham for one-on-one politicking Confederate style, to make sure Pelham knew that he, Appleyard, was Pelham's "man" at the Regiment.

"Do you, by any chance, have a bourbon, somewhere, I could 'borrow?' " Appleyard had tipped his glove. He would milk the Pelham connection for everything he could get.

"No, I don't."

Appleyard questioned the reply with a frown.

"Well, maybe one of the supply guys has an extra." Appleyard was never without a back-up resource. "I'll get one from them."

Potter questioned Appleyard's timing and location for a cocktail party; he also questioned Pelham's thirst this early in the game. He kept both questions to himself. If "J" wanted to go for it all, that was "J's" move.

Appleyard returned, his offering for Pelham in hand. He began packing his knapsack for his sortie; then he asked an improbable question. "Are you going to wear those store-bought boots of yours up there in the front line—those sissy L.B. Bean boots?"

"They're L.*L.* Bean boots. And yes. I wear them every-where except in the sack. If that's a problem for you, I envy you. My problems don't include what other officers wear on their feet. Again, that's *L.L. Bean.* Got that?"

Appleyard grumped in back-countryese about Reserves and their fancy-dan get-ups and choices of non-issue gear, and departed the tent.

What will "J" say to Pelham when he sees Pelham's Gokey boots, Potter mused? Let's get professional here and decide what Pelham really needs in support.

He laid the edge of a graph paper sheet across the map quadrangle showing 884, and pencil marked the quadrangle borders. He placed dots on the graph at each elevation contour line of 884's north scarp, then transferred the elevation numbers to the corresponding graph paper lines outlining the contour of the scarp. It gave him the profile, the cross section of Pelham's aerie. The front of the scarp appeared too high and too steep to be protected by friendly artillery; the trajectory of artillery shot would carry beyond into the valley below. Artillery could not protect Pelham's immediate front line from a North Korean mass crawling up to attack.

Colonel Kluck agreed. "Let's call the artillery right now and tell them about this."

The colonel hung up his phone. "Well, you heard it, too. They say they could hit the slope, but final protective fire would drop 'shorts' onto Pelham's people, which neither Pelham nor his people would appreciate. We'll have to move our mortars much closer behind Pelham. Thank you for looking into that, Captain. You're going up there in the morning?" A statement more than a question.

"Yes, Sir. I should be on top with Pelham by 0830. Captain Appleyard has already left. He'll meet Pelham tonight."

The colonel's silence and stare said more about his opinion of Appleyard than Potter expected to be given.

"Well, I'm glad someone let me know where my Operations Officer is spending the night."

More silence, then, "Captain, you call the heavy mortars. Use my name, and tell them I want a full section of those guns on the move by first light. Pelham better forget the Hollywood stuff and get ready for serious fighting. Call

Division and see if they can't match our contribution with more four-deuces. They must have some extras somewhere."

"Yes, Sir."

Potter called the heavy mortar people, got the reply that he asked for the impossible. He responded emphasizing his authority and the special issues present, and recommended an end to the argument. He concluded the call after extracting understanding and agreement.

As he packed for the morning ride and climb, he thought Appleyard's head may be in the clouds up on 884 with Pelham and a bottle of bourbon, but down here his ass is in one big-time jam! I think I'll take the best from Appleyard's playbook, and bring an offering of my own. If Pelham isn't thirsty, I'll bring it back. Here it is, a fifth of "Old Tennis Shoes;" Old Tennessee at a buck twenty-five. I can spare that.

*   *   *   *   *   *

Potter caught his breath from the climb and followed a path along the frontline bunkers. When he found a nonchalant private cleaning his rifle, he asked directions to Captain Pelham's Command Post.

"On the forward slope about a hundred yards along, Captain."

The forward slope! Where else? Looking Kobiyashi right in the eye, the way his great-grand daddy looked across at U. S. Grant from time to time, once upon a time! 'Way to go, Pelham!

Potter found Pelham seated next to his bunker, inspecting Kobiyashi's lines through field glasses. The valley between him and the enemy had filled with mist during the night. The NKPA's ridge top floated above the mist blanket.

"Captain Frank Pelham, I presume."

"Captain Potter of the First Marines, I believe. I declare I am overwhelmed, I say overwhelmed by the attention I am

receiving from you all. Do sit down and rest from your hard
climb. You must be all tuckered out!"

"You do pick the highest ground for yourself, I must say.
And those field glasses didn't come from supply, did they?.
Did Great-Grampaw pick them up at Manassas or the
Spotsylvania?"

"Neither. A cousin liberated them in Jena, Germany; Carl
Zeiss' best. Here, take a look. One of those goddamn ani-
mals is cooking his breakfast next to that big bunker, on the
left just out of the mist."

Potter focused the field glasses, exclaiming over the
brightness and definition of their image. "I'll be damned!
I think he's having Cream of Wheat. No, it's Quaker
Oatmeal!"

"It's unpolished rice out of his extra stocking, or someone else's stocking. What's up, Doc?"

"Out of the kindness of his heart, as we speak, Colonel
Kluck is placing a section of four-deuce mortars in your
immediate rear, at your exclusive beck and call. The forward
observer should be along shortly to register such protective
fires as you may require. Does that not make your day,
Captain?"

"Well, it does, and it does not. Is there something in the
wind?"

"Not for sure. Your opponent may be getting goosed to
do something about you, and he may be getting his own
native urges to make a run at you. 884 belonged to him until
three months ago. What I just told you *is official* advice."

"I read you loud and clear." Pelham put his field glasses
back to his eyes. "I read you loud and clear. I had to sack the
artillery forward observer. He couldn't seem to read a map,
or he didn't want to have to read this particular map. The
new guy isn't here yet. I hope your guy works out better."

"He'd better work out better. If he does not, call me or
Colonel Kluck anytime, day or night, rain or shine. I'll tell
the colonel I promised you that. The artillery can't shoot
close in final protective fires for you, without your getting

more than your share of the fire—the short rounds—which we didn't think you'd enjoy."

"No, I—we—would not. The artillery sent an air observer to look over the opposition yesterday. He flew so close to the NKPAs they shot at him with something that sent him home early for lunch. He can't help at night, anyway."

"Are the Labor Troops—the yobos—keeping you in food and drink...I mean water?"

"Yes. They're doing okay."

"Bullets, replacement weapons, whatever?"

"Yes. Speaking of drink, did someone tell Appleyard he could come up here for a 'Lost Weekend?' "

"No. He's supposed to be liaisoning with you. Why? Where is he?"

"Sleeping it off."

"What?"

"Yeah. We settled down after he got here last night, had maybe two each. Then he goes after the bottle as if it were the last he'd ever see. He had so much so fast he passed out cold."

Potter looked at Pelham. Neither spoke. Appleyard had blown his politicking venture into little pieces. He would be a long time replacing the opportunity.

"I can replace the 'Old Tennis Shoes.' It's in my pack. Did he give you any trouble?"

Pelham shook his head. "Not a chance. Not a chance one. Want to walk the line with me? It's that time of my day."

"Lead on."

Potter followed Pelham along his Company front, four hundred yards of ridge top. It commanded a horizon-to-horizon view of North Korean mountainscape. Shellfire had cleared the trees and brush off the top of Kobiyashi's ridge, the nearest ridge. His bunkers showed clearly as big, rounded piles of dirt and gravel, the gun ports in each shadowed by the low sun.

Potter listened to Pelham's estimate of Kobiyashi's route of approach. "He'd probably move his troops out through

that notch in his ridge on his left. It's close to that spur running out from this ridge. That's where he'd direct his
columns to come up at us. He'll wait for the dark of the
moon or a rainy night."

"What does he have behind his ridge?"

"Mortars. His direct-fire guns are on the ridge behind
him. They fire at us over the low stretch on the right. I'll put
the artillery to work on them when the observer gets here,
or I'll call it in myself."

"Does he have any heavier stuff, like 122s?"

"If he has, he hasn't shot them at us."

"Have you been in touch with the Air Wing? They could
go over whatever is on the reverse slope over there."

"I can't control the bombers. I'll shoot the artillery first,
as soon as the new observer shows up."

"To repeat, call me or Colonel Kluck if you don't get the
artilleryman you like, or the bombardment you want.
Colonel Kluck is fishing for another section of four-deuces
for you, also. Do feel free to call us collect."

"Count on it, Captain Potter, Sir. Count on it!"

"Here's the 'Old Tennis Shoes'—for *your* consumption.
Don't down it all at one sitting."

"Thank you, kindly, Captain, and I shall not. Shall I tell
Captain Appleyard you inquired after his health?"

Potter thought for a few seconds. "If you can get around
it, don't tell him I know he over indulged. Let him worry
about it and see how he handles it. How about that?"

"My lips, I say, my lips shall be sealed."

"Keep your guard up, way up."

"I shall. Thanks for the help."

Potter saluted and started down the reverse of 884.

*   *   *   *   *   *

While driving his jeep, Potter began outlining to himself his
report to Colonel Kluck. He had decided not to mention

Appleyard's free-fall unless questioned directly. His only first-hand knowledge would be Appleyard's absence from his meeting with Pelham. If questioned about Pelham's report, he would answer in full. He did not want to "rat out" Appleyard. He didn't need to put him down deeper; Appleyard had done all his own digging.

Colonel Kluck sent for him to report. Potter reported Pelham's composure, his grasp of the terrain and its threats and strong points. He had accepted Kobiyashi as a particularly dangerous opponent, and sent his thanks for the added firepower supplied by the colonel. He reported observing the heavy mortar people digging gun pits and readying to go into battery. Adding to the telephone lines dropped from yesterday's helicopters, linemen had begun climbing straight up the pitch to connect with Pelham's rear. Their radio jeep had also been dug in, showing only its antenna whip above ground.

"I got him another section of four-deuces. They are on the road and will deploy as our mortar company directs, under our orders. Photo-reconnaisance will fly over Pelham's front tomorrow morning and report what they find soonest. You say there is a delay in getting an artillery observer to Smith? I'll fix that when we're through here."

The colonel ended his advice, and looked carefully at Potter.

Here it comes! Easy does it, Captain Potter.

"You'll have to cover for Appleyard in any problems Pelham brings to us. He gave you high marks, and I promised him your full attention any time he needs help. Appleyard can handle any odds and ends that need doing. You handle all Pelham's requests until relieved. I'll tell Appleyard when he gets back; he is not to be in touch with Pelham until further notice from me."

Then Colonel Kluck identified Appleyard's angel. "His father is a state representative in Tennessee. But he's connected to the state's U.S. congressman. I've got to keep him. I cannot send him forward to a rifle company. I cannot. And

I can't up and fire him. In the meantime, you take good care of Pelham. That's all, Captain."

"Yes Sir."

Back at his desk, Potter asked for messages and received something unexpected. "A dogface—I mean an Army—Major called you from Division Intelligence, a Major Shroyer. He said he'd be there until 1600 today with their G-2 people."

"Patrick! Long time no see, no speak! I've been here so long I'm picking up the language. What are you up to here?—a career of espionage? I see, Specialized Foreign Studies." Potter listened to his friend's guarded explanation of his duties.

"Here's one you may be allowed to answer. We're up against a General Kobiyashi here. He's a renegade Japanese. He worked for Emperor Hirohito until Hirohito closed up shop. Have you crossed his spoor on any of your expeditions?

"Jesus Christ! We'll treat him with due respect. Great to hear from you . . . Take care. It's rough out here."

Potter repeated to his sergeant what Shroyer had told him about Kobiyashi. "When the Japanese Army surrendered in 1945, the Army Commander for Korea sent a colonel ordering Kobiyashi to disarm his command. Kobiyashi shot the colonel with his trusty Nambu, beheaded the corpse and sent the head back to the Army Commander. Then he ran off and joined the new North Korean Peoples Army. This gem will make Pelham's day if something else hasn't already."

After supper, the colonel sent for Potter.

"Appleyard will stay with Pelham again tonight, voluntarily, with Pelham's okay. He tried the old food poisoning lie, which Pelham called him on. If Pelham can put up with him, he can stay. I don't need him nursing his 'food poisoning' down here. Pelham has his new artillery observer and the mortar observer in place. Nothing else to do until tomorrow. Anything on your mind other than the North Korean Peoples Army?"

Potter repeated his friend's report on General Kobiyashi.

"Well, if we ever get him cornered, we won't send anyone under a white flag to take his surrender! Thank you for the bedtime story, Captain. See you tomorrow."

*   *   *   *   *   *

Potter, Colonel Kluck and the entire Headquarters woke up to heavy incoming artillery landing west of the Regiment's left front. All hands scrambled to telephones and radios. Division artillery responded with counter battery fire within minutes, both sides increasing fire as minutes passed. Potter's staff remained at "stand to" as the barrages continued. The crashing incoming on their left and the rapid fire thumping of the friendly counter-battery fire reminded the staffs of the huge firepower each side could turn on or off in a moment's notice.

The Command and the staff tents had been surrounded by sandbags stacked to shoulder height. They would protect their occupants from near misses; the tent tops would get shredded by flying splinters and debris. A shell landing inside the sandbagged tents would shred the occupants, and the occupants all understood this.

"Well, he isn't going after Pelham; but the night is young and dark. They're doing a lot of shooting but no reported movement. What's your guess, Captain?"

"They can't just shoot to shoot. They don't have the ammunition. They started at 0145. They should make a move, if they plan to, no later than 0215. If they don't, it's a diversion."

At 0230, guns on both sides continued rapid fire. Colonel Kluck called Pelham.

"Nothing to report here, Captain. I assume you're all on full alert? Good. We'll keep you advised. You do the same with us. In fact, you call me every ten minutes on the ten minutes starting at 0240. Don't be bashful. Every ten minutes starting at 0240. Over and out."

"He says 'all quiet.' "

"Maybe the diversion is for someone further west, away from Pelham."

Pelham called at 0240 and reported "all quiet."

At 0245 the colonel and Potter both jumped at a heavy, rapid artillery barrage landing on the right front, Pelham's front.

"Here comes the samurai! Get through to Pelham, if you can. Get through to the four-deuces if you can. I'll call the artillery and the reserve battalion. Everybody move out. Move out!"

The telephone line to Pelham had been shot out. His radio channel still came through clearly, overriding NKPA jamming.

Pelham to Potter: "We are receiving direct fire from 76s to the right front. Reconfirm my request to artillery for everything they have to shoot 854, the southwest face." Pelham repeated the request with map coordinates, and Potter relayed it to the artillery. They acknowledged the request from Potter and from Pelham's forward observer, and advised ranging shots had been fired.

Kobiyashi began firing something onto Pelham much heavier and louder than 76s. Potter asked Pelham what he thought it was.

"Estimate 122s. Repeat: estimate 122s falling in rear. We are boxed in by 122s targeting rear! Can observe muzzle flashes due north. Will give compass bearing from here. Cannot—I say again—cannot estimate range!"

Colonel Kluck took it calmly. "If those are 122s impacting his rear, they're being fired from Manchuria! Those are flat shooting guns. They can't drop shells over that high ground, and Pelham couldn't see their muzzle flashes! Let me talk to Pelham."

The colonel brought Pelham up and told him to get a compass bearing on the flashes, and get the best count he could of the seconds elapsed between the muzzle flashes and the sound of the guns, if he could hear the guns. Pelham sent a compass bearing within minutes. The "sound ranging" took minutes longer. Then Pelham estimated seven seconds "flash to crash."

"9800 feet—3300 yards from where Pelham is! Those can't be 122s! Kobiyashi's gotten himself howitzers from somewhere! Joseph Stalin doesn't sell howitzers! What is he shooting? Potter, tell the artillery I want the 210s on them, whatever they are. They can figure their position close enough from Pelham's data. The 210s will rattle them enough so they'll shut down. How are the four-deuces making out?"

"One gun knocked out."

"Bring up Pelham again!"

"Recon, how are you doing? Flares on your right? Call for final protective artillery, or I will. You tell me."

"Pelham doesn't want artillery close in. The mortars have held them down the slope."

Minutes later, "Pelham says the 76s and the 122s have ceased fire."

More minutes later, "He says small arms fire from his front has stopped."

"Tell the artillery to keep punishing them! Rub Kobiyashi's nose in it!"

More minutes. "Pelham reports his right intact. He also reports, 'The guy from the orchard is hurt.' "

Colonel Kluck relaxed and went on to the next piece of business with Potter.

"Go up there tomorrow and see how Pelham is personally. If Appleyard is still there, hold his hand for a while and make sure he gets evacuated. Mainly, get Pelham's candid appreciation of the fight. Get his casualty count, and what weapons caused them. He may not say everything he wants to say in his official After Action report.

"Get somebody over to Pelham's rear, to where he said 122s impacted, to pick up shell fragments and get them to Ordnance to look at. Tell Pelham he gets air strikes soonest whether he likes it or not. Kobiyashi can't be over-served. I'll bloody him so good he won't test me again."

A relaxed and confident Colonel Kluck, almost smiling, nodded at Potter. "I am rid of Appleyard! I am rid of the spy! Get some sort of details from Pelham about Appleyard 'volunteering to remain at the front without regard for his own safety or his painful wounds, standing firm in harm's way throughout the fight.' Then get Appleyard into medical treatment long enough to earn his Purple Heart. You write a citation for him based on what Pelham says, or make it up. But don't overdo it. I'll send the congressman's boy spy back to Division. Tell personnel I want another Operations Officer, one who can hold his booze and his tongue. I'll get you a citation, too, but you've got to stay here with me. That was a good night's work. Well done, Captain Potter."

Potter went back to his office, relieved his sergeant for the night, or until another alarm. "Write Appleyard's citation, his ticket to the rear. The yokel is out of here! I guess this is where I sit down and put my feet up on my desk and let it all sink in." Potter felt flattered that Colonel Kluck had confided in him. Relaxed after winning another fight, the colonel's instructions to him, his choice of words, enunciation, presence—native or learned—showed how well he had been educated at "the trade school," Annapolis. He had never let on to Potter what he thought of Appleyard or the other Appleyards sent to work for him. He had kept a straight face when Appleyard questioned him, the colonel, about the adequacy of artillery support, and his, Potter's, intelligence and initiative and energy vis-a-vis Kobiyashi's dispositions. At the time Potter thought Appleyard had overplayed his hand, again. He had only overplayed his Daddy's hand—again.

Pelham had had his "near run thing." So had everyone. Aside from the casualties, not all that much to this fighting stuff. Always give The Boss more than he asks for. Always let him know where you are and what you're doing for him! Answer phones politely and clearly. Not much to it at all.

He had received a package from home, unopened in the excitement. It included a ten-ounce medicine bottle filled with Wild Turkey cushioned, disguised, in copies of *The Wall Street Journal*. He thought of his mother going to a medicine cabinet, selecting a bottle of a certain size that would be a gift that might be shared, but not large enough to touch off a Dionysian festival. Potter could see her rinse it, give it to his father, who would charge it with Wild Turkey, package and mail it.

Potter felt too wrung out to celebrate. He put the bottle away in a pocket to savor later. An enclosed letter from his father remarked about how infrequently news came out of Korea, and guessed the front had to be quiet; the quieter the better. He called attention to the growing firmness in utility security prices, and suggested Sam move part of his portfolio into that category. The rest reported family news and best wishes, with a P.S. from his mother, which did not mention the illicit gift.

The securities advice moved Potter to take up the *Journal* and compare his holdings' performances with the market and with the utilities his father mentioned. He liked packaged goods shares, but accepted the wisdom that utilities had a strong future, especially if producers got the handle on nuclear-generated power. His father had included an addressed return envelope and paper. Potter began a letter reporting 'all quiet,' agreeing with his father to move his Kraft Foods and General Foods into whatever utilities looked most promising. He did not mention Colonel Kluck's promise of a citation or medal.

10

Contestants and Complications

JUNE 25, 1950 – JULY 27, 1953
TO THE PRESENT

The Korean "conflict" or "police action" began June 25, 1950 with the North Korean Peoples Army assault into South Korea. The attack took the UN by political and strategic surprise. The U.S. and fourteen other United Nations members undertook to fight it within geographic and political limits, often blunting or canceling the industrial and technological muscle in the UN members' arsenals.

The Republic of South Korea had not prepared for an invasion. It organized its Army as an internal security force. One-third the size of the attacking NKPA, its Army lacked armor, air, adequate artillery and field training. As the fighting escalated, U.S. advisors were assigned to train Republic of Korea (ROK) conscripts pulled in from shops and rice fields. Neither spoke the other's language. It would take most of the three-year war to bring the South Korean Army up to enemy standards of training.

South Korea was not the only unprepared combatant. The UN did not anticipate having to "reverse their field" from the Communist menace in Western Europe to rescue a faraway Asian polity considered by U.S. military planners to be "not strategically sensitive."

None of the U.S. services had prepared to fight this war. The newly created free-standing U.S. Air Force had not fully equipped itself with state-of-the-art tactical or strategic assets. It had bought heavily into the second and had committed more of both to Western Europe's defense. It could not use nuclear weapons with political safety because of possible Soviet overreaction to their use against allies.

The Marine Corps had been gutted to two skeleton divisions. The U.S. Navy's air arm, its most powerful surface asset, had to fight an inland war, never being offered a traditional, sinkable adversary. U.S. armored forces were of limited use in mountain country after they had, early on, blown away the outnumbered North Korean armor. The traditional U.S. ground forces, lacking the glamour of other service forces, became the "varsity team" in a war decided by firepower delivered the old-fashioned way.

The UN ground forces would also be politically con-
strained to avoid heavy casualties while fighting armies,
North Korean and Chinese, profligate with their most
potent asset, their own troops' lives. The two Asian powers,
always outgunned in artillery weight and numbers, and
harassed by unopposed air power, could sluice their "human
sea," continually replacing their field armies' losses from
unlimited, uncomplaining censuses.

Butcher's bill items for the Sino-Korean gamble eventu-
ally included 1.5 million Chinese and North Korean military
casualties. Chairman Mao Zedong's oldest son would be an
early Peoples Liberation Army casualty. U.S. casualties
totaled thirty-seven thousand dead and one hundred thousand wounded. South Korean losses included two hundred
seventy-five thousand Army casualties dead, wounded,
missing or captured and pressed into the North Korean
army. Two million Korean civilians died as direct or indirect
casualties of the fighting.

A Chinese Communist Forces tactical axiom boasted
"two legs beat four wheels." It meant that CCF infantry on
foot deploying anywhere in the countryside, over any terrain, could outmaneuver enemy infantry riding in used-up,
out-of-gas trucks strung out on North Korea's sketchy road
networks. It didn't anticipate having to beat bulldozers that
built roads anywhere any time, and Detroit's flood of new,
gassed-up "six-by-six" trucks. The Sino-Korean logistic sys-
tem consisted of "cargadors," coolies on foot, carrying loads
of supplies, repairing roads and bridges all night and hiding
from UN air attacks all day.

Battlefields fall to whoever controls the initiative, to
whoever selects the field and the timing of the battle. North
Korea accomplished both in the summer of 1950, charging
two hundred miles over U.S. and South Korean forces,
stopped only a few miles short of winning its war.

The CCF accomplished the same the following winter,
intervening massively and by surprise, almost shattering the
UN forces. The first two near-victorious attacks caught the

U.S. militarily and psychologically unprepared—and mis-led. The newly arrived CIA's warnings not believed, ground and aerial reconnaisance reports gathered, noted, then cavalierly misjudged and dismissed by the U.S.' megalomaniac, hallucinating Theater Commander.

After a year in Korea, the UN forces' flesh and blood and weaponry, with competent leadership, had bombarded the CCF and the NKPA into an unaccustomed, entrenched stalemate. Both armies held chains of ridge tops and hilltops where the fighting became Chinese or Korean small units facing UN small units, on North Korean geography.

The United Nations' intervention kept the South Korean nation intact. The U.S. and the UN joined the unwanted game on the unexpected field, unprepared, distrustful or denied the use of many of their assets. They rescued and stabilized their ally militarily, politically and economically.

The war remains a 50-year truce.

South Korean Army soldiers weigh an average twenty pounds heavier and stand three inches taller than soldiers in the North. The per capita income in the South is ten times that in the North. Weekend recreational automobile traffic between South Korean provinces rivals U.S. interstate resort traffic. Ruled by the son of the dictator who decreed the 1950 war, the xenophobic North lobs ballistic missiles here and there and tinkers with nuclear fireworks, while its people dine on rice and cat and dog meat.

The NKPA field equipment compared favorably to Czarist Army equipment: cloth caps instead of helmets, no first aid packets, zero air support, bolt action rifles (sometimes captured Imperial Japanese Army issue), Russian submachine guns and Degtyarev automatic rifles, and World War I vintage Maxim machine guns. They were strongest in 82mm mortars, Russian artillery designed for use on Russian steppes, not in Korean mountains with minimal telecommunications. They wore baggy mustard-colored uniforms and rubber "tennis shoes" instead of field boots. Infantrymen carried rice rations in bags shaped like socks.

Undernourished and seldom taller than five feet, hill folk dragooned and conscripted from secluded mountain farms and villages in North Korea, wherever accident placed them, the NKPAs fought on familiar terrain and made skilled tactical use of it. They were hardy, tolerant of privation and discomfort, resourceful engineers and bold, tenacious fighters.

*   *   *   *   *   *

UN forces occupied Hill 854 until the truce of 1953. Published maps of the Demilitarized Zone indicate it is a permanent point on the Demarcation Line between North and South Korea. None of the North Korean territory was retaken for purposes of political liberation, or mineral or commercial exploitation. The only economic resource captured during the fighting described here is the area now designated the Sorak-san National Park. The park advertises lodging and outdoor activities, seasonal hiking and nature walks and skiing.

ORDER INFORMATION

Copies of *Tent Pegs and 2nd Lieutenants* can be ordered directly from Conversation Press, Inc., from Amazon.com or through your local bookstore.

You may call 1-800-848-5224 or fax 847-441-5617 with your order and Visa or MasterCard information.

You may also mail your check (made payable to "Conversation Press, Inc.") or your credit card information, and your order to:

Conversation Press, Inc.
Box 172
Winnetka, IL 60093

A single copy of the hardbound edition of the book is $19.95, and the paperback edition is $13.95, plus $3.00 for shipping and handling. Illinois residents should add $1.55 (hardbound) or $1.08 (paperback) for sales tax (or enclose your sales tax exemption number).

Call 1-800-848-5224 to inquire about quantity discounts beginning at 10 copies ordered, or for shipping charges on multiple-copy orders.